Going Solo

Going Solo
Developing a Home-Based Consulting Business from the Ground Up

William J. Bond

McGraw-Hill
New York   San Francisco   Washington, D.C.   Auckland   Bogotá
Caracas   Lisbon   London   Madrid   Mexico City   Milan
Montreal   New Delhi   San Juan   Singapore
Sydney   Tokyo   Toronto

McGraw-Hill

A Division of The **McGraw·Hill** *Companies*

6 7 8 9 0   DOC/DOC   0 1 0

ISBN 0-07-006642-6 (pb)

ISBN 0-07-006641-8 (hc)

*The sponsoring editor for this book was Allyson Arias, the editing supervisor
was Penny Linskey, and the production supervisor was Pamela Pelton. It was
set in Fairfield by Priscilla Beer of McGraw-Hill's Professional Book Group
composition unit.*

Printed and bound by Donnelley/Crawfordsville.

McGraw-Hill books are available at special quantity discounts to use as
premiums and sales promotions, or for use in corporate training programs. For more information, please write to the Director of Special
Sales, McGraw-Hill, Professional Publishing, Two Penn Plaza, New York,
NY 10121-2298. Or contact your local bookstore.

This book is printed on recycled, acid-free paper containing a
minimum of 50% recycled, de-inked fiber.

*To my mother, Mary E. Bond, who showed
me how to be a good parent, and stood
by me when I needed it. You're the
best, Ma. I love you.*

Contents

Preface

There is an exciting business opportunity awaiting you in the challenging world of your specialty consulting business. During the last few years, you have learned a great deal in your career field; it might be in the area of software, business systems, education, writing, speaking, selling, marketing, computer graphics, transportation, human resources, quality control, diversity training, advertising, desktop publishing, Internet marketing, personal financial training, and many others. You can sell your valuable experience and knowledge for excellent fees. Your clients will pay you thousands of dollars for sharing your information with them. In return, your specialty consulting saves them time and money.

Your most important obligation to your clients is to treat them with respect and learn the consulting process so you can serve them with the highest quality possible. One successful consultant from Massachusetts said, "Pick the right specialty, learn it fully, and become competent enough to help your client." The goal of this book is share an insider's view of the consulting process and to motivate you to keep practicing your specialty until you become the best in your field.

You will have the best of both worlds: the satisfaction of owning your own business, whereby you can make an important contribution to your client, and the luxury of operating the business right out of your home. This book shows you how to operate your home-based business with the highest degree of professionalism so you can keep growing your business into the best in the field. This guide to success shows you how to manage your business so you can market yourself to your specialized target market, how to develop successful selling, writing, and presentation skills, and how to price your services.

You will also learn how to match your skills to your specialty field and develop a line of services and products to become a million-dollar consultant. You have the ability and the skills to make it big in this business as your own independent consultant. You are the manager of your life and your business, and when you nurture client-consultant relationships, look out for the rights of all your clients, and build referrals with your finely tuned networking system, you will become the best consultant in your field. You will become an industry celebrity with your appearances on the radio, and television. Magazines and newspapers will interview you, and you will speak at various clubs and organizations. You will learn how to discover and develop consulting opportunties long before your competition. You will learn how to evaluate your work, and how to keep improving it, so you can make a profit on each assignment and on each client. Let's get started and let's enter the exciting world of consulting together. We have no time to lose.

William J. Bond

Going Solo

WHY YOU CAN BE SUCCESSUL IN SPECIALTY CONSULTING

Success! Your own consulting business can be one of the most exciting and profitable businesses of the 21st century. You will be offering a unique service to your clients: your own special knowledge, advice, and information. You are needed. Your client will expect you to help solve the problems in your specialized field. In this exciting book, you will learn how to choose your own best possible specialty field. Then you will learn how to use the consulting process. The consulting process includes developing a set of services to market to your preselected client base or target market and then delivering the best possible consulting services so you gain customers as well as future opportunities to expand your business. By helping your customers succeed, you're helping yourself succeed.

Specialty consulting is not without competition. You will find competition in every specialty consulting field from small-business consulting to computer-systems consulting. This competition will motivate you to select your very best specialty field and then learn why your client will choose you in the first place. Just as you go through a buying process when your purchase any product or service, your potential clients will go through a similar, perhaps more expanded, process before they hire you to help them. For example, Howard, a specialized consultant from Massachusetts, found out after he was accepted as the consultant of choice for a high-tech company that he was one of eight other candidates in the consulting search project. To survive and prosper in your specialty field requires that you run your business as a professional business, with the skills of an aware, knowledgeable, and goal-driven entrepreneur.

WHAT IS THE KEY INGREDIENT FOR SUCCESS IN SPECIALTY CONSULTING?

In one word, *competence* will bring you success. Your clients will hire you when they feel you have the skills, talents, and competence necessary to help them. Your chief responsibilities will be to put yourself into the shoes of your client, focus on what is needed to attain the assignment, and then follow through successfully. Competence means asking some important questions. What is the problem? How can you solve it? Why should they hire you? The more you examine and answer the questions that are relevant to your client, the better job and services you can deliver. Competence means knowing not only your specialty field but how you can use your skills, talents, and abilities in the best interests of your client.

Like all skills, becoming competent requires some trial and error in order to develop fully. For example, Dan from New Hampshire specializes in helping small businesses deal with keeping unemployment costs in line. When Dan first started his home-based specialty consulting business, he expected to learn the business quickly and expand the business rapidly. However, Dan found that his clients did not make decisions quickly and that it would require making stronger, more persuasive presentations and working closely with future clients to sign them up. Dan increased his competence by learning the process of obtaining and keeping clients, and he is now enjoying an excellent, lucrative consulting business.

WHAT IS THE HISTORY OF CONSULTING?

Consulting has been with us for centuries. When kings, queens, and other dignitaries needed expert advice on a subject, but lacked the time or decided not to exert the effort themselves, they would call in the consultant. Once the queen hired the consultant and the problem was solved, the consultant was free to go on to another client or customer. The queen was happy because she solved a problem, avoided hiring a full-time aide, and kept her budget in order. Over the years, consultants have played an increasingly stronger role in today's businesses. Today's business owner, the entrepreneur, knows that to run a business in the 21st century will require specialized knowledge and skills. It will be too expensive to hire someone full time, so a specialized consultant can come to the rescue, analyze the problem, solve it, and keep the client happy. In this way, business can be developed in the future.

You will be successful as a specialty consultant when you realize that you have a business, and it requires sufficient revenue or sales to make it profitable. One-shot jobs and quickly developed assignments, with little if any follow-through, will not serve to build your business, but rather slow it down and make it harder to develop it fully. This is similar to Dan's experience in his consulting business. Your focus should be to accept assignments which will enable you to carve out a top reputation by delivering the best results possible. You develop a top reputation by working hard to deliver the best possible results, by looking at the problem in a unique way, by analyzing it fully, and by keeping your client's best interests at heart. Your client is not just a name or a number in your account files, but the raw material with which to build your future business. The more assignments and experience you get from a client, the easier it will become to deliver quality work and the best results in the future.

WHAT IS CONSULTING?

The term *consulting,* or *consultant,* is overused and often misused. In the simplest form, consulting is giving advice to someone. When you expand this definition, a consultant is an expert who specializes in a specific field and gives advice, counsel, and related services in that field for a fee. The key words in the second definition—*advice* and *fee*—are crucial to your success. Your advice must be correct and relevant to the assignment at hand. In short, you must be right. Your work and advice are not given free; you charge a fee for them. Too often, consultants lose valuable clients because they fail to charge them or they charge them too little for the consulting work. Your services and advice are valuable, or the client would not have even considered hiring you in the first place. As a specialty consultant, you sell advice and you sell services. When you give them away for free, you will set yourself up for failure. One of the key goals of this book is to offer you unique ideas to market your services and advice so you can get paid fully.

To give you a better idea of what I'm talking about, the next time you shop for groceries, fill your shopping cart to the brim. Then, when you get to the checkout aisle, tell the cashier you want the food for free. Simply say, "I want this free." You will be laughed out of the store and possibly out of town. The store owner is an entrepreneur just like you, and he or she must pay for the food, pay the employees, and pay the rent, lighting, and heat. As a consultant, you have bills to pay to run your business. Charge and collect for your services.

WHAT IS SPECIALTY CONSULTING?

Specialty consulting takes place when you focus your sights, energies, and activities on a specific interest or field. For example, Paul from Delaware specializes his consulting activities and services on governmental contracting, showing his clients how they can obtain government business and what paperwork is required to succeed. When a customer asks Paul about private business contracting outside of his specialty area, Paul listens to the request, but informs the customer that his specialty is governmental contracting.

Restricting your business to a specialized consulting field helps both you and your client. You will have a clear focus to specialize in only one area, and you can do a better job with a limited research area. The client will get quality information from a specialist, can use this information right away, and can get the maximum investment from it.

I enjoy the comments from Bob, a consultant from New Jersey who specializes in the human resources area. Bob helps businesses successfully run their human resource departments, the personnel departments which hire and train their people. Bob said, "I will only take an assignment that I want and feel I can do well." When I asked why he didn't take an assignment in order to increase revenue and gain experience, Bob said, "I will get more assignments when I can do my best work, in a specialized field, and keep my client happy with my results." The quality of your work is your ultimate product.

THERE ARE VARIOUS MARKETS OR CUSTOMERS FOR YOUR CONSULTING BUSINESS

Not long ago, I directed a home-based consulting seminar and was asked, "How is the small-business market for consulting these days?" My answer: "This is a good market, but try not to restrict yourself to only one market of small business." For example, once you develop a set of skills in a specific specialty, such as compensation consulting, you can offer it to smaller, medium-sized, and even large companies. By trying each market—small, medium, and large—you can then decide which one will work best for you. Later, I discuss how you can develop those valuable skills, techniques, and consulting tools to deliver the best possible services to the largest possible market.

LEARN TO USE YOUR TIME EFFICIENTLY

The specialty consultant business depends on the most important stock in trade, the most important resource of all: *time*. You have only so many hours of billable time to earn your revenue. If you work 52 weeks per year, 5 days a week, and bill 8 hours per day, you will be able to bill for 2080 hours. In the beginning of your business, you must work hard to get appointments and make presentations to get consulting assignments. You will be doing research work after normal working hours to maximize your time.

Successful specialty consultants learn that proper priorities are essential to achieve the best results for their clients and their business. A specialty consultant from Maryland, Kathryn, finds that her practice is growing steadily by focusing on her lifelong priority: to be the best consultant in the direct marketing field. Kathryn uses each day as another opportunity to move closer to this goal.

Kathryn makes a list of things to do each day and tries to include items which will help her make contributions to the most important people in her professional life: her clients. She wants to be the best possible time manager so she can make her time work for her each day. One goal of this book is to help you use your time to reach your goals for success.

LEARN THE PROCESS AND MANAGE YOUR RESOURCES

As the entrepreneur, the owner, the manager, and the director of your activities, you have the power to steer yourself into the winner's circle. You have this power because you direct your resources, and your ultimate goal will be to give more to your clients than they expect from you. Once clients realize that your business delivers more than the competition, you will establish a profitable base.

Too often, consultants as well as other business owners expect to succeed without delivering the best possible services. The best services result from thoroughly learning the consulting process: from setting the assignment, to researching the problem, to presenting the best possible solution or idea. This book works hard to teach you the full process.

PROMOTE YOURSELF TO SUCCESS

You will be successful when you learn to promote yourself and your services to clients or potential clients. You will learn to write news releases telling others of your activities and successes so they can hire you in the future.

Promotion is more than just advertisements in your local paper or trade magazine. It includes public relations, which is the best possible way to become known in your specialized market. This book shows you the best methods and techniques to get interviews in print publications, how to get on radio and television shows, how to appear on cable shows and perhaps even start your own cable show. The opportunities for promotion are limited only by your imagination and the effort you make to get your message across to others. Let's sum up.

SUMMARY

You can be successful in your own consulting business. Specialty consulting is an exciting business once you select your best field on the basis of your own skills, interests, abilities, and experience. You will succeed when you show others that you have competence. Learn the history of consulting in your field of interest. Study your competition. Focus on the two key words in consulting: advice and fee. Charge appropriately for your advice. Focus on your specialty; keep yourself informed of new developments and trends and always learn as much as you can about your field. Get to know your market and how to obtain the largest possible share of the market. Use your time wisely; time is all you possess. Learn the process of consulting fully; it will become easier the more you learn about it. Learn by doing. Promote yourself to success.

Now let's turn to the skills you possess and can deliver to your client to build a solid foundation for success in the specialty consulting business.

DO YOU HAVE WHAT IT TAKES FOR YOUR CLIENT TO HIRE YOU?

This chapter helps you focus your marketing skills and sharpen your expertise to reach your clients directly. The reasons clients will hire you involve the same considerations made when they evaluate your services. Think about the reasons they should hire you, and never lose the opportunity to favorably promote yourself to a client. For example, if you're hired by the ABC Company to help market their new product to retail stores in California, this may be the crucial point in the evaluation of your work. Remember to keep your end result in mind at the beginning of your business.

Following is a list of criteria which your client will use to evaluate you and your services:

THE CRITERIA YOUR CLIENT WILL USE TO EVALUATE YOU

YES	NO	
____	____	Did the consultant focus on my problem?
____	____	Did the consultant take the time to get familiar with my business field and competitors?
____	____	Did the consultant see the problem in his or her own way?
____	____	Did the consultant look at the alternative problems sufficiently?
____	____	Did the consultant involve me and my ideas, goals, and plans in the problem-selection stage?
____	____	Did the consultant make the experience a partnership or form the perspective that you "shot from the hip" to finish the assignment?

____	____	Did the consultant act like he was paying his own fee?
____	____	Did the consultant give sufficient time to each step in the consulting process?
____	____	Did the consultant consider the changes in the business world in performing the work?
____	____	Did the consultant take sufficient time and effort to learn about my company or organization?
____	____	Did the consultant show what was wrong, but fail to properly fix it?
____	____	Did the consultant get sidetracked into other areas to the detriment of the assignment at hand?
____	____	Did the consultant save us the money she promised in the initial meeting and agreement? If not, why not?
____	____	Did the consultant use flexibility and brainstorming ideas to reach meaningful results?
____	____	Did the consultant work well with others within the company to get the best results?
____	____	Did the consultant follow through on the work, as discussed in the process?
____	____	Did the consultant finish the project on time?
____	____	Did the consultant make a meaningful presentation of the results of the work project?
____	____	Did the consultant give the best value for the time and money spent?
____	____	Did the consultant answer questions during the final presentation?
____	____	Did the consultant use language I understand?
____	____	Did the consultant work to implement the findings of the consulting project?

_____   _____   Would I hire the consultant in other projects in the future?

_____   _____   Why would I hire this consultant in the future? Answer below:

_____

_____

_____

_____

Why would I not hire this consultant for future work?

_____

_____

_____

_____

These questions are just some of the points your client will consider once you complete your consultant project or assignment. In some cases, the evaluation might be informal, whereby the client and other employees will discuss your performance. In other cases, the discussion of your work will be more formal, whereby the client will discuss specific areas of the consulting process. This is similar to an employee evaluation, and one to which you should give full consideration and involvement. Try not to take the evaluation too personally. You are just starting out. Be willing to listen fully and don't let an evaluation devastate you, especially in the beginning of your business because you will improve as you gain additional experience.

Put yourself in the position of a client and consider the last two questions, which discuss whether or not you will be rehired. Your answers here are very important because they will focus on your skills, talents, and abilities. They may also reflect some of the areas you feel need more work to help you become a better specialty consultant. Your answers will be used later in the book when we deal with choosing the best possible consultant field to utilize your full set of skills, talents, and abilities.

YOUR CLIENT WILL HIRE YOU TO STATE AND SOLVE THE PROBLEM

The client in Minneapolis is a retail sporting goods store and finds that sales in the store are declining substantially. This problem is not entirely due to the store's employees. The client can choose what he thinks is the problem and try to solve it alone or hire you as the consultant to state various potential problems which might cause the decrease in sales. The sales decline could be due to many different factors such as poor location, poor sales help, poor inventory, poor marketing, poor public relations, poor pricing, poor customer service, poor return policies, and many others.

As the consultant, you have the opportunity to review all relevant facts in the consulting project. You are in charge of this project. The client can work with you, but you now have this responsibility to get the results. You are now in charge of finding the best way to state the problem. The best consultants know how to state the problem in the most concise and understandable manner possible. Get into the habit of listing as many problem statements as possible on a sheet of paper, in your word processor, or on your computer. In addition to listing many problems, write out the possible solutions as well. Consultants cannot just assume that the answer will appear after sufficient time and effort have gone into it. Nor can you make assumptions about the problem or the solution just because of what your client thinks might be problem A and solution B. You are not ready to make that decision yet, much like a physician who will not disclose a medical condition until the full examination and test results are available. Your success will be the result of taking the time and effort necessary to "diagnose" and state the problem fully, and then determine the possible solutions to fix the problem completely.

YOUR CLIENT HIRES YOU BASED ON THE BENEFITS OF YOUR CONSULTING SERVICES

Your client will think long and hard before a contract or an agreement is made for your services. The client must feel that the benefits of your services are worth the fee that you will be paid. Here is a list of some benefits you can offer to your clients.

BENEFITS YOU CAN OFFER CLIENTS

_____ Your competence

_____ Your interest in the field

_____ Your time-management skills

_____ Your educational background

_____ Your experience in the field

_____ Your research in your specialized field

_____ Your experience with other clients

_____ Your organizational skills

_____ Your experience with similar consulting projects

_____ Your analytical skills

_____ Your diagnostic skills

_____ Your listening skills

_____ Your information-gathering skills

_____ Your computer skills, including Internet skills

_____ Your ability to analyze problems

_____ Your low overhead

_____ Your writing ability

_____ Your partnership skills

_____ Your publications in your field

_____ Your list of patents

_____ Your ability to add value to your findings

_____ Your awards received in this field

_____ Your ability to hold trade information or secrets in confidence

_____ Your honesty and fairness

_____ Your ability to meet deadlines

_____ Your skills in working with others

_____ Your contacts in your field

_____ Your willingness to solve the problem

_____ Your interest in finding the best opportunity for successful results

_____ Your resources to find the best information

_____ Your ability to be a team player

_____ Your willingness to spend sufficient time to succeed

_____ Your creative and flexible approach to assignments

_____ Your willingness to give your client more than expected

_____ Your objectivity

_____ Your enthusiasm and desire to help the client

_____

_____

_____

_____

_____

Check the items which you feel you offer or can offer to your clients. By focusing on your benefits to your clients, you can add these benefits to your proposals or be willing to tell your clients, "I'll meet the deadlines for you, and my experience in helping ABC Company with a similar assignment will help us succeed." Notice how you can state that the assignment is not yours alone but for the client as well.

Note also that an important benefit to your client will be your willingness to practice confidentiality on a client's trade secrets or information which might be used by your client's competition. For example, let's say that during an assignment you learn the formula to make product X. You have an obligation to keep this information to yourself so that others cannot profit from it. As a consultant, you have a very privileged position, and you must earn and guard the respect and trust the client places in you.

YOUR WILLINGNESS TO GO THE EXTRA MILE WILL BE ONE OF THE MOST IMPORTANT BENEFITS YOU OFFER YOUR CLIENT

Dawn, a consultant from Texas specializing in running sales seminars, said her benefits to her clients include "giving them more than they expect from me, to make them feel they received top value from me." Dawn makes certain that her clients give a full evaluation after each one of her seminars, and when she sees a negative trend, she tries to correct it before it becomes a problem. Spend time with the list of benefits offered earlier because in the beginning of your business you must tell your prospective clients the benefits you'll offer to them to get the best service. Once you get the consulting assignment, your benefits will speak for themselves. But until then, train yourself to promote and sell your benefits to others; this will go a long way in the future.

THE CLIENT WILL HIRE YOU BECAUSE YOU ARE AN EDUCATOR

You cannot keep your skills to yourself. Your value will grow when you share your talents, abilities, and skills with your clients. It took you years—even decades—to learn and develop your skills, so be willing to continue sharing them regularly with your client.

For example, Stacy is a computer systems consultant for service businesses in Pennsylvania, and she looks to her chief role as being the educator to her growing client list because she reads the latest information, including books and magazines on computer systems. Stacy makes certain that upon completion of a new computer system, a full training program is given to the people working the computers and their supervisors. She also writes a complete manual of the system for training new people in the future.

Stacy extends this education strategy to getting new business as well: "I spend about 10 to 15 percent of my time on promotional and educational activities. Most of my new business is from CPAs, consultants, and attorneys. I try to keep them informed about my specialty consulting field." Stacy belongs to a consulting association to get referrals for potential clients. Your clients or potential clients must be continually educated and updated on what specific services and successful results you offer them.

YOUR CLIENT WILL HIRE YOU BECAUSE A PARTNER IS NEEDED

What is a partner? A partner does not necessarily mean the owner of a business where profits and investments are the most important consideration. In the specialty consulting business, your client may need you as a partner to explore a new idea or to research the opportunities in a new business area. A client may even ask you questions to discover better answers or uncover new information that will help find the key to success.

Your success in this people business will be your ability to make your partnership work. It might mean being an information broker, which involves supplying information to help your client. Your success lies in being the partner who will find and bring the information to your client at the right time and the right place. There is no limit to the information available today; the crucial factor is presenting essential information to help your client solve a problem, find new opportunities, or make the best possible business decision. As a partner, you have the resources to reach these important goals.

YOU ARE HIRED BECAUSE THE CLIENT NEEDS YOUR SKILLS, TALENTS, AND ABILITIES

Clients know that, in this age of specialization with its lack of time to get everything done, they turn to you to help them examine and work in a specific area. If they try to do it all by themselves, their results may be limited by insufficient facts and by information which is too old or unrelated to the problem or opportunity at hand.

Your experience in the computer field will help your client decide on the best possible computer system to help automate the business office. Your expertise in finance and investments will help your customers make the best decision on placing their money in areas which will give the best return on their investments. For example, Brian is a consultant in personal finance in New Jersey. He helps his clients decide where they should put their investment money to work. Stocks? Bonds? Mutual funds? Money market funds? Penny stocks? Brian asks his clients or potential clients the following questions:

- How much money would you like to invest?
- What is your weekly or monthly amount to invest?
- Do you need money for sending your children to college? When?
- Are you interested in retirement? When?
- Do you own a computer?
- What software do you currently use on your computer?
- Have you used programs such as Quicken or Managing Your Money?
- Do you own a home?
- When do you plan on buying a home?
- Do you invest for the short or long haul?
- Are you willing to invest for the long haul—at least 10 years?

Once Brian receives the answers to these questions, he develops a plan for his clients, and then along with the plan he details how clients can become their own accountants and consultants by following their investments closely with a personal computer. By learning and monitoring their investments, the clients can turn the computer into a teacher, bookkeeper, investor, advisor, secretary, and broker. Brian gets hired by many clients because he is willing to give seminars to teach people the basic principles. He then charges them to set up a plan, and still gets additional business by counseling and helping others who need help in the future. Brian's philosophy is simple: get as many clients as possible in the beginning and they will increase in value as time goes on.

YOU WILL BE HIRED BY YOUR CLIENT BECAUSE YOU KNOW AND USE THE POWER OF INFORMATION

There is a tremendous amount of information available today from areas as diverse as foreign sports to microbiology. Your client does not want you to make assumptions on what are the right questions and answers. Your client will hire you to discover the right information and then analyze it fully to get the best possible value from it.

A successful specialty consultant from Florida, Sharon, who specializes in interior design, said, "My job is to gather information, which is really similar to a raw diamond, which must be shaped, cut, and cleaned so that it will really shine. Information must also be gathered, shaped, used in specific areas so it will do the best possible job."

Recognizing the value of information and its proper use are probably the most important challenges for you in this business. You are really in the business of making information count in the lives of your clients.

SUMMARY

Look at your end results in the beginning of your business. Give the client reasons to hire you. Each client will evaluate you at the end of each consulting session. Review how you feel you will be evaluated. Your key benefit is your ability to solve problems. Your consulting services will succeed when you know the key benefits you offer to others. Give your client more than he or she expects. You are an educator. You are a partner to your client. Learn your client's needs by asking good questions. You must know and use the power of information. Now let's get your home-based office ready for your successful business.

GETTING YOUR HOME OFFICE ORGANIZED

One of the most important roles you will play in your consulting business will be to help your client succeed. Your most important initial challenge will be to follow the necessary steps to organize your efforts and turn out the best work possible. You need to set up the best home-based office possible to create the kind of work required to develop the best possible reputation. Take the example of Theresa, a home-based consultant specializing in certification for manufacturing businesses, who needs a home office which will house all the information she needs to help her clients. Theresa uses a separate room where she can make full use of her computer, technical software, and all the other information she needs to succeed. You should choose an office at home which will meet your needs as well as help your client.

MAKE A LIST OF WHAT YOU WILL NEED

Review the items you will need to complete your office. I like the comment of a veteran specialty consultant who said, "I need only a phone, Rolodex, and a PC, and that will do it." You will be spending a great deal of time in your office, so it will be very important to make it as comfortable and efficient as possible. Here are some items you may need:

Desk
Calculator
Computer or word processor
Copier
Phone

Fax

Chairs

Answering machine

Air conditioner

File cabinet

Bookcase

Supply cabinet

Trash can

You might not need to buy all of these items. This is only an illustrative list, and some items may already be in your home ready for use in your office. Take the example of Joe, an investment consultant from Florida. When he started out, he used the fax machine at his local business service company, and instead of buying a copy machine, he used the one at the local mall. There is no need to spend all that extra money to outfit your office by immediately buying this equipment. Purchase only the essentials now, and you can fill in the other items later.

REVIEW WHAT ITEMS YOU HAVE ON HAND RIGHT NOW

What furniture which is not being used right now can be used in your office? For example, you might have a spare desk in the basement, you might have a desk chair or other chairs in your attic, or there might be an empty bookshelf in a spare room. Match the list of items needed with the items you currently have on hand that can be used in your home-based office.

Consider buying some used furniture rather than spending excessive cash when beginning your business. There will be additional expenses, such as stationery, business cards, and permits, so if you can save on furniture, take advantage of it. As you begin your business, you will find changes in what's needed, and you can then plan accordingly.

CHOOSE THE BEST POSSIBLE SPACE OR ROOM FOR YOUR HOME-BASED OFFICE

Most people have all their rooms occupied, so if you cannot find a spare room in your home, review your living area for a possible space, such as in your basement, your attic, or a section of your little used family room. Choose a location that is as far away from the noise and energy of your living quarters as possible. For example, Donna, a home-based taxation consultant, decided to set up her office close to the phone in her kitchen. But there were many interruptions which continued until she moved her office into her finished basement. Once you choose an area, try to spend time there each day, even if it is only to read some mail or send a letter to a potential client. Get into the habit of going to your office. Measure the space in the room or the living area. Now measure your furniture and draw up a layout of where you want your desk, bookshelf, and computer located. Figure 3-1 shows a possible home office layout, which will give you some ideas.

Place the furniture in the best possible places and try it for a few days. Focus on efficiency rather than appearance in the beginning stage. You will find that minor adjustments can make your office more comfortable and efficient for you. As your office takes shape, you will then be able to add the paintings or pictures on the

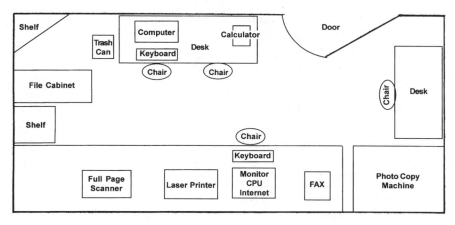

Figure 3-1 *A home office layout.*

walls and the other small details that personalize your work area and bring it to completion.

BUY A GOOD DESK AND CHAIR

Your desk is one of the most essential pieces of furniture in your entire office. If you cannot afford a good new desk, buy a used one until you can afford the best desk possible, because your work will be done at your main desk.

Your chair must support you for many hours and days at a time. Choose one with casters to help you wheel to other parts of the office and select one with the best possible support for your back. One consultant from New Jersey said he tried to get by with an inexpensive used chair but found himself going to the doctor to treat his bad back. Choose the chair that gives you the full support you need.

YOUR FILE CABINET KEEPS YOUR RECORDS OF CLIENTS

Keeping the best possible records of your clients and the work you have performed for them is essential. In addition to these records, the file cabinet will hold accounting information to help you keep score of your business financially. It also holds the new information in your specialty field. Make it a point to clip and file relevant articles on new developments in your specialty field and file any information you find. Successful consultants know the value of keeping the information that will help their clients.

Your file cabinet will hold information on potential new clients. What businesses are growing in your specialty field? Which ones can use your experience and knowledge? Clippings from newspapers, trade magazines, or meetings with others in the field can give you the kind of information that can help you turn potential clients into fee-paying clients. Take the time to discard outdated papers from your file cabinet and keep your information relevant and up-to-date. This will save you time in the long run.

LEAVE THE TIME-WASTER EQUIPMENT OUT

Leave the television and the VCR in another part of the living quarters, apartment, or house if you find them distracting. Paul, a medical services consultant, was forced to move his VCR out of his home-based office when he continued to play tapes of his favorite television shows. The radio is popular because it can be enjoyed while focusing on your reading, writing, or computer work.

WELL-PLANNED, QUALITY STATIONERY AND BUSINESS CARDS SET YOU APART

As a specialty consultant, the most important marketing leads will be generated from your letters or getting your business cards into the hands of the very best possible clients. Some consultants find that a business card can inadvertently set up a networking chain. For example, one person tells twelve people, and each of them in turn tell twelve more people. Some consultants have a logo designed. Such artwork or a distinctive type arrangement on your business card or stationery can set you apart. Figures 3-2 and 3-3 present examples of business cards.

Once you establish a letterhead layout for your business card, you can use it for your stationery, letters, proposals, contracts, or

---

Janet Z. Lucina
Interior Design Consultant

101 Main St.   707 372-1091
Elyria, Ohio   FAX 707 372-1040

Figure 3-2 *Basic business card.*

Home-Based Business, Time
Management, Job Skills

William J. Bond

Author, Speaker, Consultant

---

67 Melrose Avenue
Haverhill, MA 01830
508-372-7957
508-858-6791

Figure 3-3 *Multiple fields business card.*

other forms you intend to use. The same letterhead should appear on everything you mail or give to potential customers.

HAVE A RUBBER STAMP MADE SIMILAR TO YOUR BUSINESS CARD

Sooner or later, you will run out of stationery, and before you can order it from your printer, you will need to send out a letter to a client. Rather than waiting for the printer, simply and quickly apply your name, address, consultant specialty, and phone number to a sheet of paper using the rubber stamp. Rubber stamps are inexpensive and can save you time and effort.

KEEP SUPPLIES STOCKED IN YOUR OFFICE

Adequate supplies are essential to help you do your best work. Here are common supplies needed to round out your office.

SUPPLIES NEEDED

Stapler and staples   Mailing envelopes

Files   Color markers

Pens and pencils

Stationery

In and out boxes

Ruler

Post-it Notes

Datebook

Rolodex

Dictionary and thesaurus

Scotch tape

Folders for presentations

Computer paper

Wite-Out (correction fluid)

Paper clips

Postage stamps

Letter opener

Legal pads

File folders

Scissors

Inventory your supplies regularly to avoid running out just when an important meeting or presentation is due for a new or potential client. There are many national office supply stores which sell reasonably priced supplies especially geared to home-based businesses.

SELECT A BOOKCASE LARGE ENOUGH FOR YOUR NEEDS

Your bookcase will be an important part of your consulting business because you need to know the history of your specialty field, what is happening now, and what it will be doing in the future. Use your bookcase to hold your specialty books, and when it fills up, make space by throwing out the books or printed materials you no longer use.

GET THE NECESSARY BUSINESS PERMITS

Check with the clerk in your town or city hall to determine what permits or licenses are needed to operate your consulting business at home. Since you are not operating a retail store, there will be few, if any, clients or potential clients coming to your home. Check also with your attorney to make certain that you have obtained all of the permits to operate in your area. Once everything has been processed, you can start your consulting business, which will include managing consulting projects, working with your clients, and running your profitable business.

YOUR ELECTRONIC HOME OFFICE IS LESS EXPENSIVE TO EQUIP THAN 5 YEARS AGO

We live in a very competitive business world; many products are improving and the prices are getting lower and lower. To give you an example, you can currently purchase a printer/fax/copier and a desktop computer with a hard drive, CD-ROM, fax modem, with speakerphone and voice mail for $3300. This same equipment in the year 2000 will sell for between $1800 and $2000. Take advantage of the special prices to make your work more professional and save yourself a great deal of time and effort.

Take the example of Rebecca, a public relations consultant with a Los Angeles–based firm who wanted to spend more time with her children and decided to start her own home-based consulting business. Since her home-based office is computer oriented, she is turning out very professional work from home. "My computer system at home is as good as the one at my former job. I get to see the kids more often, and do not miss the 2 hours of commuting." Turn your home-based office into the best work space possible for you.

CHOOSE THE BUSINESS ORGANIZATION BEST SUITED TO YOU

There are three different ways to set up your office:

1. Your *sole proprietorship,* whereby you as the entrepreneur are the sole investor in your business. As the sole owner, you reap all the profits during the profitable times, but also assume the responsibility for the losses when and if the business suffers a loss. The chief advantages of this organization are the speed with which it can be set up and the rewards you receive from the profits. The

chief disadvantage is the unlimited liability for losses or problems which can result from this business or any other business as well.

2. The second organization is a *partnership,* whereby you and another individual sign an agreement to invest $5000 each and agree to split the profits on a 50-50 basis. The agreement also states that your partner will concentrate on the selling of the consulting services and you will focus on the consulting projects and the day-to-day meeting with clients until the work is completed. This form of organization is favored for the sharing of skills, talents, and expertise but still has unlimited liability for all partners for losses to the business.

3. The third form of business organization is the *corporation,* whereby you have shares of stock issued to the owners and are regulated by the laws for corporations in your state. Check with the secretary of state at the state office building in the state capital for the forms, expenses, and all necessary paperwork to set up a corporation. You should contact your attorney to ensure that you comply with all of the requirements for the corporation. The advantage of the corporation is that your personal liability is reduced, but the disadvantage is the paperwork and cost for the corporation as your form of business organization.

GET INSURANCE AND ACCOUNTING HELP

Since you will be advising clients and working closely with them, check with your insurance agent to know which insurance will protect you and your assets. Some consultants protect themselves with a liability policy to prevent unnecessary exposure to client lawsuits. Your insurance agent can direct you to the best possible decision.

Your accounting records will give valuable information to help you determine if your business is making a profit or a loss. There are four basic entries which you must record to keep your accounting records up to date. They include sales or revenues in your business, purchases made for your business, the cash received from all other sources, and the cash paid out for the operation of your business. If you have experience in accounting, you might be able to handle the beginning accounting responsibilities yourself. Once you get started, turn it over to an outside accountant, who will be able to show you the accounting information you need to manage your business. After 6 months to a year, the accountant will be able to tell you the following:

Your total sales

Your total expenses

Your profit or loss

The number of customers

What customers were profitable

What customers were unprofitable

Your total assets and liabilities

Your net worth

Whether your business is growing

What needs to be done to increase your business

A projection of sales, expenses, and profit for the next year

What equipment, marketing, and management techniques you will need in the future

How much money you will need to operate for the next 6 months

USE YOUR SPACE OR OFFICE EXCLUSIVELY FOR YOUR BUSINESS

Make certain that your office is used or can be used 24 hours each day for your business. Your office cannot be used to serve food, iron clothes, watch television, and perform other household duties for part of the day and then function as an office for the rest of the day. In order to take the office as an at-home tax deduction, you must be able to prove to the IRS, if requested, that the space is used solely for your home-based consulting business.

YOUR HOME OFFICE OFFERS YOU DEDUCTIONS

Now that you have determined that your home office must be used for your business 7 days a week, 24 hours each day, you are ready to hear about the tax deductions for your business.

If you use one room in your apartment or home and you have four rooms of the same size, you can only deduct 25 percent or 1/4 of certain deductions. Let's say your electricity bill for the month is $200. You can only take 25 percent of that ($50) for your deduction (0.25 × $200 = $50). The same principle applies to your heating costs, real estate taxes, interest on your mortgage insurance, and depreciation on your home. Check with your accountant to make certain these deductions are taken correctly.

Here is a listing of the most common deductions for your consulting business. Read each one and examine the descriptions of each following the list so that you can make the most of all the deductions:

DEDUCTIONS FOR YOUR CONSULTING BUSINESS

A. Advertising

B. Bad debts

C. Car expenses

D. Commissions and fees

E. Depreciation of assets

F. Employee benefits programs

G. Insurance

H. Interest

I. Legal and professional services

J. Office expenses

K. Pension and profit sharing

L. Postage

M. Printing

N. Rent and lease

O. Repairs and maintenance

P. Research

Q. Seminars and training

R. Supplies

S. Taxes and licenses

T. Travel, meals, and entertainment

U. Utilities

V. Wages

Deductions are recorded on your income statement.

A. ADVERTISING. This is the nonpersonal promotion of your consulting services in your business. Examples include the advertisement in your trade magazine or newspaper, the brochures you printed describing your business, the letters you mailed to your clients and potential clients, and the cost of a Web page on the Internet.

B. BAD DEBTS. Also called uncollectible accounts, these are clients who cannot or refuse to pay you for your services. You must make an effort to collect the obligation, but if you find it cannot be collected, you can write it off to bad debts.

C. CAR EXPENSES. You can deduct mileage for traveling to clients and potential clients or travel relating to the operation of your business, such as going to the post office. Keep a log of all business-related mileage and try not to mix business mileage with personal mileage.

D. COMMISSIONS AND FEES. You hired a salesperson to help you attain more consulting work and the charge is $100. You can use this deduction in your business under commissions and fees.

E. DEPRECIATION OF ASSETS. You purchased a computer system for $2000 and you expect it to last 4 years. You can deduct $500 for each year for the depreciation of the asset. The formula is $2000 $\times$ 0.25 = $500. The IRS offers guidelines for depreciation of assets, or you can check with your accountant.

F. EMPLOYEE BENEFIT PROGRAMS. Once you hire employees, you can deduct any cost related to the benefits you offer, including retirement or insurance programs.

G. INSURANCE. The insurance premiums you pay for your business can be a very valuable deduction. They include car insurance, homeowners' insurance, and liability insurance.

H. INTEREST. The interest you pay on loans and interest charged by vendors can be used as a deduction.

I. LEGAL AND PROFESSIONAL SERVICES. These deductions include fees paid to the attorney, accountant, and other professionals you hire in your business.

J. OFFICE EXPENSES. The office stationery, envelopes, folders, staples, and other expenses, such as cleaning the office, needed to maintain your business can be deducted.

K. PENSION AND PROFIT SHARING. The cost relating to the pension and profit sharing for your employees is a deduction.

L. POSTAGE. The cost to send out mail, proposals, fundings, sales materials, and checks to pay your bills can be deducted. Keep postal receipts.

M. PRINTING. You can deduct the cost of printing brochures, business cards, office forms, proposals, and stationery for your business.

N. RENT AND LEASE. The cost to rent or lease the furniture, computer, and air conditioner in your office can be used as a deduction.

O. REPAIRS AND MAINTENANCE. This deduction includes the repair and maintenance of your business equipment, including faxes, computers, audiovisual equipment, and other assets. It may include the painting and papering of your home office area.

P. RESEARCH. The cost to engage the services of individuals or companies doing research in a specific specialized area is a deduction.

Q. SEMINARS AND TRAINING. You can deduct the cost of programs you need to attend to keep current in your specialized consulting field.

R. SUPPLIES. Computer disks, fax and computer paper, and any other material you need to operate your business can be deducted.

S. TAXES AND LICENSES. The taxes paid to the state, local, and federal government and any fees for business licenses are important deductions.

T. TRAVEL, MEALS, AND ENTERTAINMENT. This deduction includes the cost associated with selling your services to your clients. Keep receipts of all items paid by cash.

U. UTILITIES. The telephone, heating, and electricity costs associated with your office space are important deductions.

V. WAGES. The gross pay for employees hired by you to work in your business can be deducted.

SET GUIDELINES AND AGREEMENTS WITH OTHER FAMILY MEMBERS

Your business will be successful when you get the support and cooperation from others within your household. Harry, an alternative health care specialty consultant as well as a single parent, is based at home and has an agreement with his school-aged children and elderly mother. He will not work in his office after 10 o'clock at night and stops working between 4 and 6 P.M. to help the children with their homework. So far, this agreement is working, but Harry knows there will be additional agreements and guidelines in the future to make and keep working at home a good situation for everyone. Share your goals and priorities with other family members; they will work with you if you let them know you love them and need their help to succeed.

Here are some guidelines and an agreement with other family members for working at home. Feel free to add your own guidelines to match your situation.

GUIDELINES WITH OTHER FAMILY MEMBERS

No working after 11:00 P.M. or before 8:00 A.M. on weekdays.

No working on Sundays.

Reward yourself for special accomplishments. For example, celebrate new clients with a small party.

Have weekly meetings with all members to discuss the next week.

Limit excessive business-related material, such as magazines, books, and articles, outside of the home-office area.

Pass along phone messages quickly and accurately to others.

Listen to and communicate with each other regularly.

All family members can help the business succeed. Benefit from their cooperation, but be able to separate work from private matters.

Respect the Do Not Disturb sign on the office door or in other parts of the home.

Respect others and their need for "space."

Address problems as they arise; regularly talk about what is working for you, and what can work better.

Ask for help when you need it.

Take the regular vacations and continue the activities you enjoyed before your home-based business got started.

Try to agree that your home is where the office is located and will require continual adjustments to succeed.

Spend one full afternoon or some special time with your spouse or significant other.

The first word in home business is *home* and will come first among other priorities.

Evaluate the guidelines regularly and add, adjust, or drop any of them.

This guideline review is important because you are doing two important things: you are preparing an office or space to start your home-based business and you are taking the time and effort to prepare guidelines to get the support of others in your family. Home-based businesses that succeed are operated by people who know the value of flexibility and of working closely with others in the family to reach their priorities. I enjoyed a comment by Calvin, a new specialty consultant from Rhode Island, "I discussed my priorities to become a top consultant with my wife, Christine, who also has a priority to become a supervisor at our local hospital. We try to listen, cheer, and support each other." This comment is important because all you can request of your partner at home is to lend interest and support to your home-based priority. It will take hard work, flexibility, and courage to keep working together to make success become reality.

SUMMARY

Your business can succeed at home. Many successful businesses were started on the kitchen table or in a spare room in the attic. Take an inventory of what you will need to get started. Make a list of what furniture you have on hand now. Match the list. Choose the best possible space, room, or area. Select a good chair, desk, and file cabinet. Leave the time-waster equipment in other parts of your living area. Purchase good business cards, stationery, and a rubber stamp. List supplies you will need. Look into the electronic office. Get the necessary permits, insurance coverage, accounting help, and the best business organization for you. You must be able to use your office area exclusively for 24 hours at a time to get the home-office tax deduction. Discuss with other family members your plans for your business and how you can work and live together as a family unit while you make your business grow and prosper.

MATCHING YOUR SPECIALTY TO YOUR CLIENTS

I have spent the last 30 years studying, researching, and writing about successful people in home-based businesses and in the world of work. Successful people work hard to do the things others avoid. They keep learning and have an important sense of themselves; they know themselves fully and keep setting priorities which impact and contribute to their lifetime priority. They know what they can do very well and find their market niche; they take ownership, responsibility, and management of their working lives. You can do the same.

Successful specialty consultants are unique because they are priority driven and want to help their clients, but they know that their success will depend on accepting projects, assignments, and work that matches their interests, skills, and abilities. It sounds simple enough, but too often, many of your skills, talents, and abilities are not taken into account. You are the manager of your skills and abilities, and you must be willing to take a periodic inventory of them and then select activities and challenges which will make full use of them.

For example, Phyllis of Vermont always wanted to get a college degree, but her life took many different directions. While raising a family, she worked in writing and illustrating children's books, started her own publishing firm, worked in wildlife management, and studied extensively about new physics. Phyllis learned her local college was offering a special program which offered extra advance credit for prior learning. This process required taking an inventory of her experiences and writing them up for the advance credits toward her college program. Phyllis finished the process and received 42 college credits, equivalent to one year and one half of college. After the process, Phyllis said, "It was hard work, but the thinking and writing taught me there was really a great deal in my life's experience. I am a better person because of it." Phyllis had an important experience of reviewing her working experiences and then writing about them to make them more realistic and relevant to her life. This is an extremely important process that all specialty consultants should consider to help them present themselves in the best possible light to their clients. You will be a better consultant when you know what interests you, what you know very well, and most important of all, when you have competence and passion in this area.

BE WILLING TO GIVE YOURSELF CREDIT

Once you research your life and work experiences and write them out, you will obtain a much better understanding of what skills, talents, and abilities you possess. In many of my home-based seminars, I quite often find that prospective specialty consultants assume they should consult in a certain field without fully examining their full inventory of potential skills. Successful specialty consultants take the time to know themselves completely. In the following inventory, answer each question fully.

Personal Inventory

- What do you do for work right now?

- If retired or out of work, what is your work specialty?

- What was your favorite subject in grade school?

- What outside activities did you enjoy in grade school?

- What subjects did you enjoy in high school?

- What courses did you especially enjoy and excel in? Why?

- Can you speak another language? Which one(s)?

- If you decided to teach a college-level course, what course would you select? Why?

- If you had today free to yourself, how would you spend it?

- What working activities do you enjoy? For example, do you like working with people, things, or ideas?

- Do you have any experience in running your own business?

- Do you participate in any activities that you can influence the results of or help others? Which ones?

- Do you assume responsibility for both the quality and quantity of your work and the work of others? Explain.

- Do you accept constructive criticism well?

- Do you keep up with the latest developments in your job or career field (e.g., magazines, newspapers, seminars, tapes, etc.)?

- What periodicals, books, and newspapers do you read?

- What activities do you participate in during your spare time?

- If you won a million dollars in the lottery today, how would you spend the money? How would you spend your time?

- In what areas would you like to spend more time (e.g., spouse, significant other, children, parents, hobbies, home-based business, sports, etc.)?

- If you started college tomorrow, what would your major be on the basis of your life and work experiences? Why?

- What are your main interests? Do you spend enough time in these areas?

Once you complete the inventory, review your answers and discover any trends that appear. For example, do you want to work with people or things? Do you want to work in a technical area or in a nontechnical area such as advertising or retailing? No one but you can choose your specialty consultant area, so you must spend the time and effort to find it. On the lines that follow, sum up the important points in your inventory summary. An example is provided.

I like working with people and numbers. I'd like to be a personal

finance consultant.

_____

_____

EXAMINE YOUR WORK AND LIFE EXPERIENCES

An examined life is an active and successful life. You must keep looking ahead in life, but continually examining what you learned and experienced in the past puts your plans for the future in perspective. Doria is a specialty consultant in computer graphic consulting, and before she picked this specialty, she completed an inventory exercise and analyzed it fully. Then she wrote out her relevant work experience from her first job out of college to her most recent job with a high-tech company. Life experiences are very relevant as well. Doria was divorced 2 years ago and is raising four children on her own. This experience has helped her set priorities for herself, such as working closely with her children, which taught her the value of communication, understanding, and respect for each other at home. These personal experiences became essential to her success. Doria has been laid off three separate times during the last 5 years because of excessive downsizing and reorganizing. She learned that being laid off is not something to take personally, but a time for regrouping her skills to the present market and looking for new work as soon as possible. Write out your work experiences and life experiences on the lines that follow. They might include entrepreneurial experiences which helped you become what you are today. Writing your experiences will help you choose the best consulting specialty possible.

YOUR WORK EXPERIENCES

_____

_____

_____

_____

YOUR LIFE EXPERIENCES

_____

_____

_____

_____

YOUR ENTREPRENEURIAL EXPERIENCES

_____

_____

_____

_____

Your entrepreneurial experience can include any activities from your early childhood when you sold girl or boy scout cookies, cut lawns, did child-sitting, washed cars, delivered papers, ran a carnival (e.g., set up a contest and sold tickets for it), or any activity in which you come up with an idea to sell a product or a service and then marketed it to a customer. This is an extremely important experience because it forces you to change your mindset from earning money by working as an employee to taking the responsibility yourself and delivering a product or a service to a customer for your own profit. This develops an entrepreneurial spirit which can help you not only in the specialty consulting business but in your whole life as well.

In a recent home-based consulting seminar, we discussed how entrepreneurial experience can improve your chances to succeed. Don from Vermont asked, "I tried a small wood stove business a few years ago and it failed. How can this experience help me?" I told Don that all entrepreneurial experience—the positive and the negative—is worthwhile, and the challenge is to focus on what is learned and apply it later to achieve the best results. You can learn from all areas of your life.

ACCEPT ALTERNATIVE WAYS TO SEE YOURSELF

Too often, when I ask people in my seminars and during consulting meetings to describe themselves and what makes them unique, they describe themselves the way their friends or family would describe them. Look beyond the stereotype description and examine how you can use your special experience and interests.

For example, take Steve, a consultant for small businesses in Delaware. He worked in the grocery trade for many years while attending high school and college, and some of his clients are in the same field. When Steve did the inventory in this book, he found that he took Spanish in high school and college, and when in the military learned to write it while stationed in Mexico. He has since developed an ability to use this important language. During a recent meeting, a client told him that one of the major changes in her business was an increase in Hispanic customers. The client decided that she wanted to develop a marketing campaign to reach this new segment. Since Steve had the ability to speak and write Spanish, he was able to make a presentation and get the consulting assignment. Furthermore, he opened a new service to sell to his clients: the understanding of the Hispanic marketing segment. Steve learned that by fully defining himself he added to the services he offered to others.

DEFINE YOURSELF

Successful consultants stand out from the crowd because they have a firm understanding of their skills, talents, abilities, and experiences. They also know what they enjoy doing, and take assignments and projects in these areas. The best consultants look at themselves as people trying to deliver the best possible services to help their clients. Here is how Sheila, a home-based consultant in telemarketing, described herself:

> I offer 10 years' experience in telemarketing, which includes training, operations, and obtaining sales forecasts for products ranging from home insulation to investments. I have taken many college classes in marketing and direct marketing, and have served on various direct marketing boards. I want to use my broad experience in the field of telemarketing to help my clients succeed.

Now, on the lines provided, take the time to define yourself and what you can offer your clients.

_____

_____

_____

_____

NOW DISCUSS THE BENEFITS YOU CAN OFFER YOUR CLIENTS

Knowing your skills, talents, and abilities gives you the information you need to discuss your benefits. For example, Susan of Baltimore worked as an administrative assistant for many years and was trained in both business and interior design. She had toyed with the idea of starting her own retail business but decided to pursue home-based specialty consulting, and her major priority was to choose an area that would suit her personality, interests, and financial needs. When you select your specialty, you must consider choosing something you really have a passion for and determine if the potential exists to earn the money you need.

Susan found that her chief benefits were her organizational abilities, her ability to work well with others, her interior design experience, and her ability to work under pressure and deadlines. After doing the full inventory, she decided to enter the interior design consulting field where she could work both with clients and other interior designers to plan and design the best possible projects.

Fred decided to choose another specialty field. He did the inventory, listed his work and life experiences, and decided that his main interests and experiences were in the area of human resources. His main concern was discrimination in the work force. Fred even narrowed his specialty to discrimination against women in the work force. Take the time and effort to narrow your choices down to the best specialty possible for you.

WHAT ARE SOME CONSULTING FIELDS?

Here is a list of possible specialty consulting fields. Look them over and choose a few potential fields of interest. From your list of two or three, narrow it down to one.

POSSIBLE CONSULTING FIELDS

Administrative	Bridal consulting
Advertising	Business development
Airport management	Business writing
Alcohol abuse	Career counseling
Apparel	Catering
Appraisers	City government
Art management	Club management
Auctioneers	Collection
Audio systems	Communications
Audiovisual presentations	Computer hardware
Auditing	Computer programming
Automotive	Computer software
Banking	Computer systems
Beauty advisor	Copywriters
Biofeedback	Cosmetics

Cost-benefit

Credit

Customs

Data communications

Data processing

Direct mail

Drug abuse

Economists

Editorial

Education

Energy management consulting

Engineering

Entertainment

Environmental analysis

Environmental control

Environmental hazards

Executive search

Export-import

Finance and accounting

Financial management

Fingerprint

Fire prevention

Food preparation

Foreign marketing

Forms design

Fund raising

Government contracting

Grants/grantsmanship

Graphics design

Health care

Health maintenance organizations

Hospital

Hotel management

Internet information

Industrial methods

Industrial psychology

Industrial relations

Insurance adjusters

Insurance advisors

Interior decorating

Investment

Labor relations

Legal

Lighting

Mail order

Mailing lists

Management

Market research

Marketing

Marriage

Meetings management

Mergers and acquisitions

Mergers and divestitures

Methods engineering

Municipal services

New product planning

Office design

Office methods

Office procedures

Organizational development

Packaging design

Pensions

Placement

Product evaluation

Public relations

Purchasing

Records and data control

Robotics

Safety consulting

Strategic planning

Telemarketing

Travel and Tourist

Video and audiovisual

Wildlife

This list is a basic list to give you an idea of the various opportunities available in the world of consulting. A more detailed list is available to you in Appendix B at the end of this book.

NOW IS DECISION TIME

Choose the very best specialty consulting field which you feel will best utilize your skills, talents, interests, experiences, and passions. Do you really want to work with people in this field? Can you talk about this field for hours without becoming bored? Do you have a good feeling about the field? Write your consulting field on the line below:

_____

By specializing in this field, your clients will perceive you as a better consultant because you have made a choice. By focusing on one specialty area, you can then take the time and effort to become the very best in this field. With the additional knowledge of your specialty field, you can command higher fees and better contracts to help you succeed.

SUMMARY

Successful consultants know themselves and their specialty fields. Know the value of your work and life experiences. Give yourself credit in your personal inventory. List your entrepreneurial experiences. Your setbacks are valuable learning experiences. Look at yourself differently. Define and describe yourself. Determine your major benefits. Review the consulting fields. Now choose the best one for you.

HOW TO FIND YOUR CLIENTS

When the subject of getting clients comes up during our seminar on home-based consulting, I take out the mirror I have on the table at the seminar room and point it toward the attendees in the audience. You must be the focal point on reaching your market and try not to delegate this important responsibility to others. You know your specialty, you learned it over the years, and you know the people in your field who will purchase your consulting services. You can use this important information to direct your energies in reaching your clients. Keep telling other people about yourself and your ability to help others. Get excited about your specialized and unique services. Blaze a trail to reach them. Educate others about what you do.

DEVELOP YOUR OWN ELEVATOR SPEECH

One way to let people know what you do is to develop your own 30-second "elevator" speech. This speech is quick but to the point, and it educates others on what you do. Take the example of Mary, a public relations consultant in Massachusetts who helps others by writing their speeches, articles, and other business communications. Here is her 30-second elevator speech:

> I am a public relations consultant specializing in helping businesses and entrepreneurs communicate better on paper. I will help you sound better on paper. Please take one of my business cards. Thank you.

Notice how Mary gave a good description of what consulting services she offered and, most importantly, how she presented the benefits of her consulting services by stating she would help businesspeople sound better on paper. Successful consultants know the value of keeping their name and their specialty in regular view of their clients or market, and you come closer and closer to success by telling others about yourself. On the following lines, write out your own 30-second elevator speech to communicate your specialty and your services.

_____

_____

_____

_____

Practice and use your elevator speech regularly. You are your own marketing manager and your own public relations manager, and it is essential that you use this speech and hand out your business card at the same time.

HOW TO REACH YOUR TARGET MARKET

You have chosen your specialty consultant field, and now is the time to match your consulting services to the best clients possible. Your clients represent a market. _Market_ is defined in the dictionary as a particular group of potential buyers. But this definition is too broad and will not work for your successful consulting business. Your success will be the result of connecting to your target market, not just the general market. The target market is a group of people who are most likely the buyers of your consulting specialty. Your success will depend on directing your marketing and selling activities to reach the target market directly. It will be like the hunter who practices with his or her rifle so a direct hit can be made to reach the goal (See Figure 5-1).

WHAT IS TARGET MARKETING?

This means that you direct your marketing activities to reach your most likely customer. For example, L. L. Bean, the founder of the

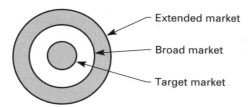

Extended market

Broad market

Target market

Figure 5-1.

very successful mail order firm which bears his name, developed a new pair of boots for the hunter. In order to sell the boots, he decided to go directly to his target market: the hunters. To do this, he traveled to Augusta, the capital city of Maine, and copied down the names and addresses of hunters who applied for a hunter's license, and he sent them information about his new boots. This example illustrates a way to reach your target market directly.

No one knows more about your target market than you. The target market might be the people who subscribe to the same magazine you read each week. It might be people who belong to your business, social, or professional organization. The target market is composed of people, businesses, or institutions, and they have a need for your consulting services. And just as important as the need, they must also have the income or the purchasing power to buy your services. Try not to confuse needs with desires. Your client A might desire some consulting services but because of low cash flow cannot purchase your services. Client B, on the other hand, needs consulting services for starting a new business, needs a consultant to develop a marketing plan, and has a deadline of September 1. Client B's need is supported by purchasing power, and $2000 has been budgeted for your consulting services to create a business plan.

Your success in the consulting business will depend heavily on your ability to research and learn as much about your target market as possible. Get to know your target market as intimately as you know yourself after doing your inventory from Chapter 4. Here is a list of possible questions you might ask about your target market.

MARKETING CHARACTERISTICS

Who is my prime client?

Where does he or she live?

What is his or her occupation?

Can I get referrals?

Who or what group can give me referrals?

What association or service group works with my market?

Does my market have enough purchasing power or capital to buy my services?

How many people or companies could use my services?

How many dollars will be spent for consulting services in my specialty area this year?

BREAK DOWN YOUR TARGET MARKET BY DEMOGRAPHICS

Successful specialty consultants know their market is more than just businesses or people; it involves important statistical information as well. For example, your market might be composed of people 20 to 30 years of age, with yearly incomes of $45,000 to $50,000, who live in the Dallas, Texas area, and are primarily women, married, but 20 percent are single. Most are homeowners. They are 20 percent Asian, 25 percent black, 28 percent Hispanic, and 27 percent white. Each statistic is important to help you reach your market. For example, if the target market has good income, you can offer your consulting services to them at a higher rate. Age is important as well. Middle-aged people will be in a better position to purchase your services than younger persons in high school or recent college graduates trying to establish their careers. Here is a list of demographics which will affect your marketing activities.

DEMOGRAPHIC FACTORS

Age	Home ownership
Income	Race
Occupation	Spouse's occupation
Age of family members living at home	Education

Sex   Geographical location

Marital status   Credit card usage

LOOK FURTHER INTO YOUR MARKET USING PSYCHOGRAPHICS

To deepen your understanding of your market, you can use psychographics, which is the lifestyle of your market. How do individuals spend their free time? Golfing? Reading books? Sports? Using their computers? Camping? Hunting? Hiking? Shopping? Listening to music? Volunteering at the local hospital or Salvation Army? Doing repairs around the house? Exercising? Working in their home-based business? Dancing? Community theater? Traveling? Boating? Religious activities? Pets? Writing? Painting? Once you discover how your market spends its time outside the working world, you can then develop new markets to help serve your consulting specialty. Here is a list of lifestyles and interests outside of work.

Psychographic Factors (Lifestyles and Interests)

Antique collectors   Wine collectors

Cable television viewers   Photographers

Volunteers   Weekend entrepreneurs

Travelers   Health food enthusiasts

Gardeners   Sports fans

Internet users

There are new psychographic groups developing regularly with people who have specific interests and are willing to spend time, money, and extend great efforts to support their interests. For example, a new marketing segment called the "21st Century Market" is a unique group of men who drive their own pickup trucks, do all the work around their houses, have their own computers and use them regularly, and work in professional jobs or own their own businesses. These individuals might be a potential target market for your business because they know the value of advice, information, and help such as consulting in maintaining their success. Your job will be to continue to review the changes in your specialty field as well as the changes in demographics and psychographics and match your consulting services and strategies to reach clients directly. Building the bridge to your clients requires a firm understanding of yourself and what you can offer them. You cannot just compete with your competition. You must defeat them convincingly.

THE COMPETITION IN YOUR TARGET MARKET IS INTENSE

Information is essential to help you succeed in today's crowded marketplace. For example, Vernon in Florida is a management consultant and he needs to set a priority to carve out a piece of the $30-billion market for management consulting services (Figure 5-2). Clients will spend billions of dollars for help in solving problems or for acquiring information to bring them success. Many large firms will be joining Vernon on the starting line in the race to capture some of this billion-dollar market. These large companies include high-tech firms that left the computer hardware business to get into software and consulting, engineering firms, computer service firms, computer graphics firms, audiovisual firms, accounting firms, and leasing firms. These companies will add to their annual revenue by including consulting as another important service to their clients.

Figure 5-2.

The six largest public accounting firms are moving into consulting because it continues to increase each year by 20 to 25 percent and it continues to outpace the growth of their regular tax and auditing services. The largest accounting firms offer services for their clients that include cutting costs, collecting money, managing their inventories, evaluating profit on products or services, and advising on the installation of computer systems to get maximum productivity. In short, they help their clients stay competitive and continue to grow well into the 21st century. Using the knowledge of their client's business, these large accounting firms are quick to include consulting as an important revenue source. I interviewed a manager of a public accounting firm who said, "Consulting is the fastest growing source of revenue for us. We expect it to increase 50 percent in 3 years."

To get your slice of the billions of dollars in the consulting pie, you must use your knowledge and experience in the field, and then package a presentation that shows your clients how you can help with their problems and opportunities in the future. For example, Nancy from California worked in finance and collection for a high-tech company specializing in the collection of government accounts. When she left the high-tech company, she knew that other companies both inside and outside high-tech needed help to collect promptly from the government and she focused her specialty consulting business to meet these needs. Good marketing means researching your clients' needs and developing a marketing strategy to reach your clients. For example, Nancy sent a letter and a brochure of her services to businesses in her area that sell to the government, and then set up an interview to discuss her qualifications in person.

Success results by following up every inquiry and response to you regarding your consulting activities. You are selling every day. Your potential clients might be as basic as the names on a mailing list. Some specialty consultants find that they can reach their market directly using a list of names of prospective clients. For example, if your clients are doctors, you can mail a letter describing your consulting services directly to the doctors in your field. Your key job will be to build your own list of clients. This list will be called your *house list,* and it includes your clients only. Keep this list in a safe place and do not loan it to others. Communicate regularly with the clients on your list and keep selling them on your consulting services. Your success in this consulting business will be determined by how hard you work servicing your clients and helping them reach their goals. Keeping a good relationship with the clients on your house list will help you build your business over the months and years ahead. Here are some potential mailing lists which will give you direct access to a specific target market.

POSSIBLE TARGET MARKETS

Attorneys	Building contractors
Business owners	College presidents
Accountants	Finance managers
Certified public accountants	Landscape designers
Nuclear engineers	Restaurant owners
Antique shop owners	Insurance underwriters
Photographers	Furniture store owners
High-tech companies	Family dentists
Wholesalers of toys	Hospital administrators
Travel agents	Bank officers
Discount stores	

Include clients on your house list who are called heavy users. These are people who spend a great deal of money on consulting services. These heavy users are willing to hire and pay for consulting services to help with projects or gather important information to help them succeed. They are an important part of your target market. Cultivate your heavy users to succeed.

USE YOUR LIBRARY TO DISCOVER AND REACH YOUR MARKET

Your local library might be the best place to start your process of reaching your target market. In addition to books, magazines, videos, CDs, and government publications, some are even connected to Internet and full of user-friendly public access computers to give you the data you need on your target market. Ask your reference librarian for help if needed and tell her or him about your consulting specialty. Get the help you need from associations' publications, directories, specific magazine articles, and books.

Match your specialty to your target market. Not every consultant will have a direct line to the target market like L. L. Bean did when he mailed a brochure advertising his new hunting boots to a list of licensed Maine hunters. Your job will be to match yourself and your services to the direct market. The consultant who specializes in human resources looks to companies who need help in this area; the consultant who specializes in political candidates needs a method to reach them to provide the help they require. In consulting, a great deal of business is generated by referrals, which simply means that people who know about you and your specialty will tell others to contact you. Remember to focus on this important referral group in your target market development.

HOW DO YOU GET REFERRALS IN YOUR BUSINESS?

Determine who will be in contact with your clients or work closely with your clients daily. For example, Susan is a transportation consultant who specializes in helping commuters find the best way to reach their workplaces daily. Rather than trying to reach the commuters directly, Susan approached small to medium-sized businesses and told them about her services and how she could offer important benefits to their employees. Susan found that the employers know the value of helping their employees save time and money in their daily commutes. When employees are frustrated about commuting, they may quit their jobs and take jobs closer to home. Employers do not want to replace good, quality workers. Susan was amazed at the excellent response she received from the employers; they even let her set up a seminar for their employees to inform them of the services she could offer. Referrals can help you reach your clients and your market. Below is a list of possible referral groups for various consulting specialities. Remember that referrals can become an important part of your business and may even become the main marketing access for your services.

REFERRAL GROUPS

Internet user groups	Syndicated authors
Attorneys	Writers and authors
Public accountants	Psychologists
Business owners	Teachers
Certified public accountants	Nurses
Consultants in other specialized areas	Executives
Consultants in your specialty	Managers
Friends of potential clients	Librarians
Family members of potential clients	Human resource employers
Clergy	Spouses
Physicians	Business associations
Psychiatrists	Chambers of commerce

FIND YOUR MARKET, RESEARCH LOCALLY, AND THINK GLOBALLY

There are tremendous opportunities to find your market today because there are computer networks of information to help you reach your market and gather information on it. With today's travel opportunities, you can travel to all parts of the world within hours. You can run an international consulting business when you have the services to match the market. Try to avoid overstating your market, but take all the action necessary to meet your market's needs. Choose the market that you can serve with the resources you possess. Now is decision time. On the following lines, match your consulting services to the market that you feel you can reach and service successfully. Avoid choosing one that has excellent potential but might be difficult to reach. Choose the one that suits you best. An example is provided.

Consulting Service	Markets
<u>Internet Consulting</u>	<u>High schools in Seattle area</u>

Notice that in the above example, the service is Internet computer systems, and the market is high schools in the Seattle area. Fred decided to choose the high school market because he has taught business on the high school level in the area, and he knows many teachers and administrators in the high schools, and feels comfortable and aware of the needs of this target market. Choose a target market in the beginning which you know well, and where you can obtain the interviews and presentations to sell your ideas. Choose one market at this time, and with experience you can branch off into other markets. Fred wants to capture the high school market first, then in the future he will consider helping other private Internet users and businesses with their Internet needs. You can do the same.

READY—NOW SET YOUR STRATEGY

Now that you have set the market for your business, think about how you can reach that market. What techniques will you use to reach your market and sell your services there? What will you do to appeal to that market? Will you direct your business to help your clients become more successful? The more you put into your strategy, the more you will get out of it. Write your strategy on the blank lines.

Marketing Strategy

_____

_____

_____

_____

SUMMARY

You are your own marketing manager. Develop your own elevator speech. Develop your own target market. Know the demographics and psychographics. The competition is intense for your market. Use your local library. Match your specialty to your target market. Learn how to get your referrals and increase your market. Study all referral groups. Select your market. Set your strategy and work your strategy. Now, let's discuss selling your services.

SELLING YOUR SERVICES TO YOUR CLIENT SUCCESSFULLY

You have selected your consulting specialty based on your personal inventory and you have discovered how to reach clients by setting up a target market and developing your own strategy. But far and away the most important information you can gather will be information to help you sell your services to potential clients and your present clients. You start gathering this information before you even make a presentation to them for their consulting business. Clients vary in many ways. Some are heavy users who spend a lot of money on consultants; others make you work real hard, pay only small fees, and eventually become unprofitable. Even when you are just starting out, you want clients who will be profitable to help you grow in your business.

KEY INFORMATION ABOUT YOUR CUSTOMERS WILL HELP YOU TO SELL BETTER

One of the most important aspects of consulting is gathering, interpreting, and presenting information to your clients. The more information you can develop on a client, the easier it will be to sell.

When we discussed the market for your specialty in the last chapter, we learned a great deal about your potential target market. Now you can examine the competition and determine how you can learn from their operations. Who do they service? How do they sell to their clients? What are their advantages and disadvantages? How do they present their services to their customers? How do they deliver their services? Do they have any new techniques or ideas which you could use in your practice? Review the strategies of your competition fully and answer these questions before you try to do any selling.

HOW DO YOU GET INFORMATION FROM YOUR COMPETITION?

You can gather information from your local or regional newspapers, magazines, or even talking to the customers of your competitors. Take the example of Ron, a Cleveland-based consultant in the trucking and transportation business. His practice tries to help small to medium-sized businesses run their trucking fleets more profitably and safely. Ron found that when he talked with potential customers many of them said they used their private accountants for help in their trucking fleet operation. Then the accountants offered sales and profit information and a breakdown of the profit or loss on each sale. After Ron learned this, he developed a new sales presentation to include many other services beyond the cost of sales and profit analysis which was offered by the accountants. Ron felt his experience and knowledge in the field, such as how to obtain permits, lease drivers to save money, and how to save money on fuel, obtain back loads, and how to run the fleet more effectively, were important to his potential target market. Ron knew that some of the best clients in the target market were being serviced by the accountants, and once he presented his line of consulting services, he could increase his profits and sales. You can do the same by reviewing your competition fully. What do you offer that your competition doesn't which can benefit your clients?

SELLING YOURSELF IS A NUMBER 1 PRIORITY IN YOUR SPECIALTY CONSULTING BUSINESS

Too often, consultants object to the word *selling* and simply expect that business will come to them without any help from their own selling activities. You are a salesperson whether you think so or not because your client or potential client knows very little about you or your services and how you can help with their problem or opportunity. It will be up to you to take each opportunity to sell and educate others about what you do. From the 30-second elevator speech we discussed in the last chapter to speaking to a potential client about yourself on the phone, you are engaging in the essential activities of proper selling. When you speak to a Kiwanis or Women's Business Owners breakfast meeting about your specialty in marketing research for small-business people, you are selling because you are educating them in your knowledge of your specialty consulting field. When you make a presentation to a potential client and discuss your experience, your knowledge of their business, and your ability to handle their problem, you are selling in the purist sense. This is free promotion to increase your sales. Selling is one of the most important steps to start and build your business, and without selling, you would be at your home-based office waiting for the phone to ring. In this chapter, I will show you how to make the phone ring at your client's office and sell your services directly.

Selling is defined as the activities which include offering a service or product for sale to potential buyers or clients. In the specialty you decided on earlier in the book, there will be people who are interested in your service but will not purchase it unless you send your message out to them by selling. Selling is not something you do 1 day each week or 1 week each month, but rather something that becomes a natural part of your style and strategy to build your clientele. You must sell services to your client in the beginning to get the opportunity to go to work and turn that client into an important and valued account. Selling successfully helps you to forge long-term relationships with clients as long as you keep building strong ties which will grow stronger down the road. For example, let's say you make a good selling presentation to the Acme Company and are offered a small marketing research assignment to check a customer's reaction to a change in the design for one of their products. You work hard to develop a questionnaire, to interpret the results, and to present your findings. The company is happy and you receive payment. This is not the end of the story but the beginning. Furthering this strengthens your consultant-client relationship. You need to keep finding ways to show your clients you can deliver the critical services that are needed to help them succeed.

SELLING IS BEING FIRED UP WITH ENTHUSIASM

Successful consultants enjoy what they are doing so much that it shows in their actions. It shows in their eyes. You can see the excitement and the presence of concentration on their specialty. I enjoy a quotation by Vince Lombardi, the famous football coach of the Green Bay Packers, who said, "If you're not fired by enthusiasm you will be fired with enthusiasm." This is so true of the consulting business that you must display your enthusiasm regularly to succeed. Look and act like a winner. When someone asks you about your business and how things are going, always let them know that things are going great and that the practice is building and growing. Diane from New Hampshire, a consultant for business systems, has a good answer for people asking about her business. She states, "Business is great, people are terrific, life is wonderful, and today is mine." Developing methods to communicate with others aids your success.

NOTHING HAPPENS UNTIL A SALE IS MADE

In every business from consulting to retail to computers, sales is the most important business function. You can have the best products or services, and even the best employees in a business, but unless you can make a sale, nothing will pay for business expenses. You can have the best resources from directories, computers, on-line computer systems, books, and magazines, but without sales you cannot earn a profit to make your business grow.

Profit is essential if you want to keep your business successful. Profit is the difference between your sales and your expenses. Your expenses will be the costs to run your consulting business: the cost of your phone, the cost of your on-line computer charges, the cost for travel to your clients, the cost of your fax services, the cost of your advertising, and the cost of your supplies. Business sales expenses are the expenses you incur to generate your sales for the business. Review Sarah Costello's income statement showing both the sales and expenses for her company.

SARAH E. COSTELLO
Consulting Services
December 31, 2003

SALES FOR CONSULTING SERVICE	$100,000

Expenses

Advertising	10,000
Utilities	15,000
Travel	7,000
Insurance	15,000
Postage/Deliveries	5,000
Printing	15,000
Professional Services	8,000
Total Expenses	75,000
Profit	$25,000

Each client will either add to your profits or, if their assignments are difficult and require extra costs, result in a loss to you. Evaluate your clients periodically to see which ones are important to keep your business growing and profitable. A consultant from Illinois found that 20 percent of his clients accounted for 80 percent of his total billing or sales last year.

SELL YOUR CONSULTING SERVICES BY TELEPHONE

Nothing beats the flexibility of selling by phone to reach your clients. You can use the call to introduce yourself, introduce your services, or even ask for an appointment to present your services and tell your full story. You can spend thousands of dollars on print, radio, television and cable television, or even on the computer Internet and not talk directly with your potential clients. The people who read your advertisement or see it on a cable television show might listen and watch but still not act. With the telephone you have the flexibility to customize your call to motivate your potential clients with important information.

You can find potential clients to call by reading your trade magazines and finding companies showing growth in your specialized field. Here are some other ideas for getting referrals:

- Ask other clients and friends.

- Offer a free article or booklet you have written or obtained in your field, such as "How to Save Enough for Retirement."

- Conduct a seminar on a topical area of your field and build your own mailing list from a list of the attendees, contacting them regularly.

- Keep informing the people on your mailing list of the benefits you offer. Never assume they will call you and offer you an assignment. You are in charge of your telephone selling.

Take the example of Doreen, a travel consultant who develops group tours for clubs, organizations, and business groups. She advertised in many different advertising media, but her results were disappointing. Doreen decided to use the telephone to educate and sell her services to her potential market. She decided she needed to develop a telephone strategy to get appointments only and wrote up the following telephone script.

TELEPHONE SCRIPT

Hello, Mr./Ms. Client. This is Doreen Stein with the Holiday Travel Associates.

How are you today? I handle all the details from booking a trip to setting up meals, getting tickets to the theater, and making sure you're comfortable in your hotel room.

We are your full service group travel company. We can handle a group of 20 to over 200 people.

This month we are offering a free special seminar entitled "Successful Group Traveling" to be held at the downtown YMCA in Nashville. It will be a full hour of ideas and techniques to make your group travel program more successful. Can I put your name down for the seminar to be held at 7:30 P.M. this Thursday night on the 23rd?

Thank you. What is your full name? Will you be accompanied by an associate? What is the associate's full name? Thank you, I will see you and your associate on Thursday night.

Notice what happened here. Doreen's strategy was to get

appointments, and to obtain them, she set up a *free* seminar to speak about the full extent of her consulting services. Once attendees viewed slides at the seminar of people having fun at various vacation sites from Las Vegas to Maine and Canada, it became easier to get orders for their individual trips.

Doreen practiced her script by calling friends and asking them to play the role of potential clients. Once the script was down cold, Doreen phoned her own list of people who had used her services in the past and then called area businesses with at least 50 employees and other clubs and organizations in the area.

Doreen learned that selling is also listening closely to her clients in order to sell them her services successfully. During the first presentation after the seminar, Doreen would find out clients' preferences, needs, and priorities and then customize a proposal to reach them. Clients and potential clients can help you sell. Part of listening is really counseling your clients by helping them to inform, articulate, and fully describe what they expect from you. To help the process along, Doreen describes how she recently helped a high-tech company celebrate a profitable year by sending a full department of 150 people to a new theme park in central Tennessee. Doreen handed out travel ideas and locations for the next 6 months to stimulate the buying decision. These real-life examples helped Doreen's clients come to a decision to purchase her consulting services.

SELLING IS HELPING THE CLIENT MOVE FROM THE MENTAL TO THE PHYSICAL STAGE

To sell your services requires a decision on the part of the client. It may be yes, no, or maybe but not right now. Your chief selling job will be to take the client through the mental stage, of just thinking about your consulting services, into the physical stage, which will be giving you the order for your services. Only you can move your client from the thinking to the physical stage, and it may require more than one presentation to accomplish it. The top salespeople in the world know that in selling and in life there will be many people who will turn you down. Rejection is common. Most sales are not made on the first try. The client is still in the mental stage and might need more information, different information, or a change in his or her personal or business situation before accepting your offer.

In the beginning of your consulting business, selling may seem overwhelming, but with experience and a thorough knowledge of your client or potential client, you can succeed. Later in this chapter, I discuss telephone techniques to obtain your initial meeting, including the full telephone script. Additionally, "Making Your Public Relations Work" (Chapter 13) offers many ideas to help sell your services and become well known in your specialty field.

Take the example of Steve, an industrial engineer with a computer company from California. After working 12 years for the company in many capacities, he was laid off during the downsizing years. After trying to obtain another job using the traditional methods, such as mailing resumes and calling for interviews, Steve was unable to get any interviews and received only a few letters from the hundreds of resumes he mailed. Steve's significant other, Sally, suggested that he look into finding a networking group of unemployed people trying to find employment again. He attended meetings and met other unemployed people with the desire and need to find other work. Steve found that many expressed an interest in starting their own business, primarily a one-person business, which could be the operation of a small store selling services, a home-based business, or a franchise. During the process of seeing the need in this group, Steve decided he would start his own specialty consulting business helping people choose a business. This is similar to a business broker, but he felt he could devote more time to the client and carefully match their skills, interests, and talents to a business. Even though Steve's background is in industrial engineering, he has been interested in business and in being an entrepreneur all his life. Steve did some advertising in his local papers but knew that steady telephone calls would help build his business for him. Here is the telephone script Steve used.

STEVE: Hello! Is this Isabelle Steinberg?

ISABELLE: Yes it is.

STEVE: Good morning, this is Steve Wright. I specialize in helping people choose their own very best business possible. I call our program "Transition to Your Own Business." Have you heard of my company?

ISABELLE: No—I don't think so.

STEVE: This service is new, Isabelle, and to introduce it to you, I will be offering a free new report titled "10 Best Businesses for the Year 2000" for all people who will schedule an information meeting to learn about our unique services. Is there any reason why you wouldn't want to learn about new businesses available to you, Isabelle?

ISABELLE: I'm not sure.

STEVE: Well, Isabelle, I have Wednesday at 9 in the morning or Thursday 1:30. Which is convenient for you?

ISABELLE: 1:30 on Thursday.

STEVE: Thanks for your time, Isabelle. See you on Thursday.

Notice how Steve discussed the benefits of his consulting services and then offered the free report for all people who would agree to an information meeting with him. Steve used Isabelle's name frequently to increase the rapport with her and then set up the appointment. Telephone selling is like all selling. It's communication with your potential client or customer, and the more calls you place, the more sales you will make for your business. Use a telephone script like Steve's or Doreen's.

SET A QUOTA FOR YOUR SALES

Top salespeople know that selling must be continuous in order to keep the business going. Set a goal to get the maximum sales. For example, Janet of Virginia is a specialist consultant helping retailers run their advertising programs. She set a quota for $100,000 in sales this year. Much of her sales will require face-to-face selling, and this requires setting up as many appointments as possible. The more appointments you receive, the more sales you will get.

Janet developed the "Calls to Make Today" schedule shown in Figure 6-1. Record each call you make, do the urgent calls right away, and check done when you finally reach the right person. After your call, determine what the interest level is for the person called. Is he or she interested? If there is strong interest, use the letter A and call back soon. When there is little or no interest, mark your calendar C or D and call back in 6 months or so. In the remarks section, write down any pertinent information which will help in future calls or during the presentation. Sometimes the cus-

U R G E N T	DATE	INTEREST LEVEL A–D	CALL YES/NO		REMARKS	D O N E
CALLS TO MAKE TODAY!						
			✓	✓		✓

NOTES:

KEY–INTEREST LEVEL
A. Strong   B. Medium   C. Little   D. None

Figure 6-1   *Daily Telephone Log.*

tomer will give information to put into remarks such as "customer will meet after Christmas," "customer wants to know the price per month," "customer knows our client, the Barnard Company; owner, Vickie Brodhurst." Use those remarks to help you earn your sales. Now is the time to sum up.

SUMMARY

Selling is an important part of your business success. You sell every day. Get the key information from your buyer. Know your competition and what they offer. Sell your benefits. Selling is your top priority. Fire yourself up with enthusiasm. Know your profit and loss figures. Each client will increase or decrease your net profit. Use the telephone to help you sell. Write your own telephone script and practice before calling on the phone. Selling is moving the client from the mental to the physical or action stage. Ask for an appointment. Set a quota and reach it. Record all calls so you can avoid overcalling some clients.

Now let's turn to the next chapter and find out how to make your first initial presentation and get the sales or the consulting assignment.

SECURING YOUR FIRST MEETING WITH YOUR POTENTIAL CLIENT

Your selling efforts should have the major priority of getting your foot in the client's door so you can meet for an initial meeting where you can get to know one another and determine how your relationship can be of benefit to both you and your client. In the last chapter, we focused on making telephone calls to your potential clients. This chapter will discuss writing letters and following up to arrange this important first meeting.

WRITE A PERSONAL LETTER AND FOLLOW UP

David is a computer systems consultant based in Worcester, Massachusetts, whose client base spreads to New Hampshire and Vermont. David has an established home-based consulting business now, having started 11 years ago. He used a method of writing a personal letter about his services, including some success stories of his clients, and discussing the benefits of hiring him. When David started out, he had zero clients; now he has all the work he can handle by using the personal letter and follow-up method. In your personal letter to a potential client, discuss your experience in the field and the benefits you would bring as the client's new consultant. If you have knowledge of the client's field, discuss this experience and indicate why this will help you do a better job. For example, when David started in specialty consulting, he worked in the field for 10 years in inventory and financial management systems and used this as his niche to fully take this market.

Below you will find a letter written by a sales training specialty consultant, Sheila Conway, trying for an opportunity to discuss her specialty and some of her services with the potential client. Sometimes you can't see the prospective client and you can send the letter to the office manager, computer manager, sales manager, distribution manager, or other employee or associate representing the client. Tell your story and ask for an opportunity to discuss your services fully.

SAMPLE SALES LETTER

Mr. Chris Goodnow
General Sales Manager
Randall G/M Dealer
506 Washington St.
Cambridge, MA 02129

Dear Mr. Goodnow:

Thank you for speaking to me last Wednesday at the small-business expo in Boston. Here is a summary of my dynamic seminar program for your sales representatives.

My sales program is called "Sales Success Dynamics" and this 90-minute seminar runs once a week for only 3 weeks. It includes the psychology of selling, the techniques for communicating, how to develop the top sales presentation, new ways to handle objections, how to ask for and get the order, how to turn the customer into a life-long customer, and how to get referrals to add to your customer list.

I plan to follow up with your sales representatives in the weeks after the seminar to assure the use of our principles and techniques and their success with our program.

I will be calling within the next few days to discuss the program with you. Perhaps we can meet soon to discuss my exciting program in more detail.

Sincerely yours,

Sheila Conway
Sales Training Consultant

Notice what happened in this initial letter Sheila wrote to her potential client. She thanked him for the opportunity to speak with him at the business meeting and then wrote about what key topics would be given in the sales seminar. Sheila concluded the letter with an idea to meet soon to discuss the proposal in more depth. The key concept is to have the initial meeting with your potential client to get the business.

The initial meeting is very important for success with your potential client. Now you can meet and talk to determine what problems or opportunities exist. You can see if there is proper chemistry with the potential client. Just because you need the business and because it would help build your business are not the only reasons you should accept an assignment. The initial meeting is often informal. It can take place in a coffee shop, over lunch, or at the local business or service club. This meeting may signal the important beginning of a close rapport with the potential client.

The first meeting can cause fear in many consultants. During our seminars on home-based specialty consulting, one of the most popular questions is how to handle the initial meeting with the potential client. One consultant at the seminar asked, "How do I handle myself during an initial meeting when the questions come up about how I expect to deal with their problem, or they ask me a lot of difficult questions which I might find hard to answer without more research on their individual business or situation?" The answer to that question is a simple one. Admit the fact that this is a good question and one which you can research more. But state that to disclose the answer right now is not the best way to handle it, and you will be happy to look into it more fully for the next meeting. Notice what happened here. You carefully dodged the question and gave the potential client credit for asking a good question, but you asked for more time to research the best possible answers.

Many consultants are too eager to get the business, and during the first meeting they offer an answer to the first question, only to find that another question is asked to which they respond with a different answer, and the process goes on and on. In the final analysis, the potential client has received a lot of answers and might feel that you provided sufficient information to solve the problem or assignment. Now why should this prospective client hire you? Where do you go from there to get additional information? By giving too many answers, you jeopardize your chances of having the next meeting, which will be the contracting meeting when you make the agreement to accept the consulting assignment.

You need time to prepare for this important initial meeting, and the more information you have before this meeting, the better job you can do. Your success as a consultant will be determined by the information you can gather from the potential clients. Permit your clients to help you define the problem. You need information from them. You need them not only to show you the problem or opportunity, but to give you the resources within their company or organization to help you succeed. This initial meeting gives you a chance to meet face-to-face the person you will be working with in the consulting assignment. You have to feel comfortable with this individual. There must be a good chemistry between you and the client. When you find yourself in a first meeting and there is no chemistry there, you must make a decision on whether or not you want to accept the assignment.

Take the example of Lance, a computer systems consultant from Connecticut. He met with a potential client based on a referral from a satisfied customer. Lance did not get a warm feeling in his initial meeting with the controller, Stan, of the ABC Company. Lance felt the controller thought he knew all the answers and would be difficult to work with in any consultant assignment. Lance did not follow up to arrange a contracting meeting because he decided against the assignment. Three weeks went by and Lance still did not call the potential client, until finally the president of the ABC Company phoned and asked Lance if he was still interested. Lance said he was unsure about it. The president said not to worry about Stan, the controller, because he was leaving the company shortly anyway. Once Lance learned this, he went to the contracting meeting and is now the consultant of record with the ABC Company. Remember to sell your service, but you alone determine which clients you will accept, and the chemistry must be right for you.

How do you get the initial meeting? The initial meetings are obtained in various ways including a referral from a friend, a former working associate, or a present client, or just by following up a telephone call or writing a letter about your services. Remember that you must sell to get this important meeting. This meeting is the foundation for your successful relationship with the customer.

Methods and Examples for Obtaining Your Initial Meeting

A. Phone the potential client and ask for the meeting to present your services.

B. Tell your potential client what you have done for other clients, or as an employee with the XYZ Company, or working as a volunteer with a nonprofit organization.

C. Ask or pay someone who knows your skills, talents, and services to make calls to potential clients and ask for an initial meeting.

D. Introduce yourself as something other than a consultant. Say, "I'm Donna Ruiz. I'm a marketing doctor. I help businesses fix their marketing program to increase sales and profits. Can we meet for just 15 minutes?"

E. "I spoke to our mutual friend, Sally. She suggested I talk briefly about how I can help you with your advertising in the trade magazines. Can we have an introductory meeting this Wednesday?"

F. "I'm Margory Castro. I specialize in medical records technology. Can I meet with you to show you how to save time and money in meeting your medical record challenges?"

G. Introduce yourself to the potential client at a restaurant, present your 30-second elevator speech, and offer your business card. Ask for this person's business card to follow up.

H. Give the potential client a free case history sheet of your success with the ZYC Company.

I. Speak at the local business club or service organization and hand out business cards at the end of the program.

J. Write a letter to the editor of your local or regional newspaper on a topic which communicates your knowledge and expertise in the field.

K. "Susan, your name came up during a discussion of growing companies in the metropolitan New York area. I am an expert in hiring the best employees to help your company."

L. "Mr. Clark, I recently heard at the Topsfield Chamber of Commerce that you might be interested in the services of an expert on employee safety programs. Can we meet on Tuesday, November 3rd for a short meeting to introduce ourselves?"

Use these methods and statements to interest your client in meeting with you so you can find out how your services can benefit the potential client and take the first steps to build the future relationship. Use your first meeting to show a beneficial partnership.

PREPARE FOR THE INITIAL MEETING

Successful consultants know the importance of a positive first impression with a potential client. Your potential clients will expect you to know something about their company or organization, and in the case of an individual, to know something about him or her. What products or services do they sell? Did you ever purchase a product from them or buy one at the store? Who are their customers? How long have they been in business? Is their company growing profitable or declining? In the case of meeting with an individual, get as much information as possible to make the first meeting successful. For example, Patricia is a psychologist specializing in helping middle-aged adults choose the best careers while using all of the skills and talents they have developed during their lives. Patricia will ask for a copy of their resume or send out one of her basic applications so she can prepare for the first meeting. Be willing to prepare fully to do the best job for your potential client.

WHAT CAN AFFECT YOUR POSITIVE IMPRESSION ON YOUR INITIAL MEETING?

Your appearance is very important to make the best possible impression on your client. Make certain you are on time for the meeting. If you are delayed by traffic or an emergency situation, call your potential client and arrange another time if possible. Dress like this is the most important meeting you will ever have in your life. Even though there is much down-dressing in businesses and organizations all over the country today, dress in your very best business suit or outfit to convey the very best business and professional image. Have enough written information with you, such as your resume and brochure, to meet again with your potential client. Strive to present a relaxed and pleasing manner. You must appear as if you would be easy to work with in future jobs and assignments. Always remember to ask for the order, and the order for this meeting is an invitation back to the contracting meeting. I enjoy the statement by consultant Sylvia Stein who said, "Thanks Mr. Broadstreet for your time. I look forward to our next meeting. I'm excited about working with you and your fine company."

KEEP GOOD RECORDS OF YOUR CLIENTS

It is important to your success in the consulting business that you keep proper records for each client. Nothing upsets a client or potential client more than having to give you information which you should have anyway to service them. Organize your own working activities so you can complete your consulting projects on time. Keep a record of each meeting or communication you have with your client. For example, you just met with Debra Saurman in your initial meeting, and it went very well. You discussed some marketing plans you had prepared for other companies and your experience in your former marketing jobs. Debra wants you to put together a proposal which will include a budget and a full media program. Now you're ready to record this into the Client's Work-in-Progress Record (Figure 7-1). Keep it up to date and record relevant information as soon as possible after each meeting.

This record is similar to the salesperson's call report, whereby each sales meeting or sales presentation is recorded fully. This keeps the client's account up to date and also lets you know how the client is reacting and using your services. For example, if you get the contract to do the consulting for the marketing plan, then perhaps they will ask you to do some sales training for the field salespeople and work more closely with them on their telemarketing program. This is your scorecard on the client. This record will

Client's Work-In-Progress Record

Date	Name of Client	Remarks	What Needs to be Done Next?	Date of Work Due
i.e. 1/2/2002	Acme Company - Toy Distributor	Met with Debra Saurman, sales manager discussed their present marketing program. Discussed my experience in doing marketing plans for distributors. Debra wants to meet for contracting meeting with a proposal.	Do a full proposal including budget, marketing plan, including advertising and all mediums, including print, radio, television, and direct mail.	1/15/2000 contracting meeting (full proposal)

Figure 7-1.

be an important tool in determining your client's satisfaction level. It will help you manage your client's account. Read it carefully before making a call to your client or meeting with your client, whether informally or formally. Having the right information is an essential tool to maximize your resources to help your client succeed. Review your record weekly, monthly, and quarterly to see that any problems are corrected quickly and keep the account on the right track.

SHOW POTENTIAL CLIENTS THAT YOU'RE INTERESTED IN GETTING THEIR BUSINESS

I recall working in a large advertising agency in Boston, and when we did a major presentation for a large chocolate candy maker, Necco, on the day of the presentation, we put a large bowl of Necco candy bars on the reception desk so it could readily be seen by our potential clients. We got the account, not because we bought some candy, but because we had the best presentation which showed them we knew their business and what they needed to succeed. Figure 7-2 shows the To-Do List that Sarina Wellfield presents to her clients and potential clients, which clearly shows her specialty and her telephone number. Remember that you must sell yourself and your specialty to succeed in this business. Now let's sum up.

SUMMARY

Keep selling yourself to get your first meeting. Write personal letters. Follow up. Choose only the clients you feel you can work with successfully. Ask for the first meeting. Prepare fully for your meeting. Make the best presentation possible. Use your client's Work-in-Progress Record. Ask for the contracting meeting. Show you're interested in helping the client succeed, and you will go the extra mile.

Now let's discuss the contracting meeting.

THINGS TO DO TODAY!   Date: _____

Urgent   Done
✔   ✔

☑ 1. *Call Sarina Wellfield your construction consultant 202 377-8001* ☐

☐ 2. _____ ☐

☐ 3. _____ ☐

☐ 4. _____ ☐

☐ 5. _____ ☐

☐ 6. _____ ☐

☐ 7. _____ ☐

☐ 9. _____ ☐

☐ 10. _____ ☐

NOTES:

Figure 7-2.

PRESENTING A KNOCKOUT PROPOSAL AT THE CONTRACTING MEETING

At this point in the consultant-client relationship, you have talked with your potential client on the phone, made a short visit to his or her office, or were referred by a third party. Now you must put together a presentation so you can get the assignment, and it will take preparation and professional skills to succeed. You are not the only consultant your potential client has called to solve the problem or perform consultant duties. Never assume that just because you were asked to meet with the potential client you have the assignment. You never get a second chance to make the number 1 impression. Studies in sales show that the buyer will judge the salesperson during the first 30 seconds after the first meeting. You will be judged on your appearance, the way you carry yourself, the amount of confidence you show, how you talk about your specialty, how you display your best personality, and how you show the potential benefits the client will receive by awarding you the consulting assignment.

WHAT IS A CONTRACTING MEETING?

During this meeting, you meet with the client or potential client and make an offer to work on his or her problem or consulting opportunity. When you do a good job in the contracting meeting, a contract will be agreed upon, either in writing or simply by oral agreement, for you to assume the assignment, and then the consulting work begins. But nothing happens until you convince your potential client to accept your offer. I like the statement of Deanna, an educational consultant from New Jersey, who said,

"Tell them who you are, what you do, and how well you do what you do; tell them how you can customize your services to them, in the most friendly and helpful way. Once you get this format down, just keep doing it and following up your follow-ups. This is how you will succeed." Deanna used a very powerful term here: *customize*. Your success in this business is your specialized focus on your field, and with this carefully honed focus, you then customize your skills to the needs and objectives of your clients. You will succeed. Deanna's statement is important not only in your contracting meetings but in all areas of your business as well.

Jay is a consultant working with businesses on how to use the Internet to help them in their marketing and research activities. Before Jay goes to the contracting meeting, he does all the necessary work to learn what is available on the Internet and how this information can be of service to his potential clients. Jay watches carefully that only the essential information is gathered to avoid information overload which will sap both time and money for his potential clients. Jay said, "I will only go to a contracting meeting when I have sufficient information on how the Internet can help them. I have even turned down some assignments before the contracting meeting when I felt I could not do my best for my client." The contracting meeting is when you formally outline what you can do for your potential client if he or she chooses you for the consulting assignment.

SETTING UP THE CONTRACTING MEETING

The contracting meeting can result from various diverse circumstances: the potential client phoning and asking you to come in, a letter sent to you requesting it, a friend or associate who referred you to the contracting meeting, a package in the mail requesting information from you, a friendly telephone call from you asking for the contracting meeting, or a fax from the potential client requesting a meeting. It will be very important that you determine the information listed in Figure 8-1 before you prepare anything for the meeting. You want to customize your resources with the needs of your client. Any mismatch and you will lose the opportunity to

---

What Information Is Needed for Your Contracting Meeting?

The date and time for your meeting.
Who will be at that meeting?
What is the purpose of the meeting?
How much time do you have to present your information?
Can you use overhead projectors, videos, and other presentation equipment or techniques?
Will there be a question and answer period? How long?
What written materials do they want you to leave with them, such as a proposal, statement of work, resume, publishing credits, references and credentials in the field, patents awarded, recognition in your field, achievements in your field, information on relevant projects and recent projects?

Figure 8-1.

get the assignment. Make no mistake. There will be a great deal of competition, and one small error can spell disaster for you.

NEVER ASSUME YOU KNOW WHAT THE POTENTIAL CLIENT MIGHT NEED

Take the time to call the client and ask specifically what is needed to make their best decision. I'm reminded of the remark by Gino, a restaurant consultant from New York, who said, "I just assumed they needed a resume and two references. Instead they needed a full proposal, and I lost my ability to compete with other consultants. I will ask for more information the next time." Gino's comment is important, and the amount of information might depend on the size of the company, with larger companies requiring more information and medium and single-owner firms requiring less decision-making information. In most situations, it will be to your advantage to give more information rather than too little. Make sure your information is relevant to your client's needs.

CALL FOR ADDITIONAL INFORMATION

Sally is a human resources consultant who specializes in hiring consulting for small to medium-sized companies. She did her initial meeting with Brad and his boss, Barbara, a week ago. There was a general discussion about her services and a brief discussion of the problem the Adams Company was having in their hiring. Let's move closer and listen to the telephone conversation between Brad and Sally.

SALLY: Thanks for meeting with me last week. I was wondering when we could meet to discuss how our services can help the Adams Company.

BRAD: Oh, you're welcome. We really enjoyed it, and it opened up many new ideas for us. My boss wants to meet again, in fact as soon as possible.

SALLY: That's fine with me. When would you like to have the next meeting?

BRAD: On Wednesday the 15th of November, around 3 o'clock. Is this alright with you, Sally?

SALLY: I will arrange my schedule to make it. Who will be there? How long do I have to make my presentation?

BRAD: Good. Just my boss and me. You can have at least an hour, more if needed. At 4:30 I have a staff meeting I must attend.

SALLY: Thanks, Brad, just one more thing. What written information do you need from me to help you make your consulting services decision?

BRAD: Oh, I'm not real sure. A resume and a proposal on how you could help us select the best sales personnel for our products at Adams. Oh, also please give us at least three references.

SALLY: You will get it. Oh, Brad, can one of the references be the high-tech company I worked with for 10 years in personnel?

BRAD: Sure. I don't see why not. See you on the 15th at 3 P.M.

SALLY: Thanks for everything. I look forward to this important meeting.

Notice how Sally made certain of all the specifics of the contracting meeting. When she was unsure of the references, she asked about using her former employer's name. By getting the answers, Sally can prepare fully for the meeting.

GET ENOUGH INFORMATION FROM YOUR CLIENT

Your performance in the contracting meeting will depend upon how much relevant information you can obtain about your client.

In many cases, you need the clients to provide information about themselves to help prepare yourself fully. For example, how many people do they employ this year? How many salespeople do they hire? What are their products? Did they earn a profit last year? How much was their loss? Is their business expanding or declining according to the industry or field? To help gain access to the information, ask your contact within the company or organization. Without it, you cannot do the consulting job.

Paul is a computer consultant in Illinois, and one of his potential clients is the Smilivant Company, which is a wholesaler of plumbing supplies. Paul's contact at the company is Leslie, and they have had several telephone discussions on how they could automate the financial accounting and full inventory for the company. Leslie and Paul's phone conversation took place late on a Monday afternoon. Let's listen to it.

> LESLIE: Paul, I'm glad to reach you. Listen, I'm getting a great deal of heat from my boss on the full automation of both the financial and inventory sides of the business. When can you put together a proposal for us?
>
> PAUL: I would be happy to put a proposal together, but as I stated earlier, I need a lot of information from you in order to select the best hardware and software programs.
>
> LESLIE: I will give you whatever you need. If we need to bring in the controller in accounting, I will do so. I need to move on this project as soon as possible.
>
> PAUL: Alright, let's set up a time to get together.

Take the necessary steps to ask the potential client for the time and information necessary to do your presentation better. Many consultants find that asking for help in the beginning of the relationship and obtaining it will set a precedent for the future. Successful client-consultant relationships do not just happen, but are forged together by working in concert with one another. In a recent consultant seminar, we talked about the client and consultant as a team, and as a team working together everyone achieves more.

THE CONTRACTING MEETING MAY REQUIRE FORMAL PAPERWORK

Many large companies and governmental agencies will send you information to complete before processing your request to consult for them. For example, an executive seminar agency in Maryland will mail out the following request for proposals (RPF) for their training programs and services. The two pages give the full details on how the proposals should be written, so they can be processed efficiently (Figure 8-2). When the agency finds that certain consultants meet their requirements, they will set up a meeting to discuss

THE EXECUTIVE SEMINAR AGENCY
101 Concordia Drive, Dixville, MD 10010

To: Interested Vendors/Consultants

From: Selection Committee of Executive Seminar Agency

Subject: Request for Proposals for Specialized Human Resource
              Management Training Programs

Date: May 1, 2005

1.1   DEADLINE FOR PROPOSALS
The deadline for full submission of proposals will be: "2:00 pm on June 30, 2005"

2.2   PROPOSAL REQUIREMENTS
    A.   Full Outline of Seminar, including full title
    B.   Audio/Visual Equipment Needed
    C.   Computer Software Required
    D.   Teaching Style Used
    E.   Resume, including all teaching experience
    F.   References

3.1   HOURLY RATES
The hourly rate will be $65 per contact hour with students. It does not include time to set up class, test equipment, and ready your seminar setting. All vendors/consultants receive same rate.

4.1   COPYRIGHTS

REPRODUCTION AND USE OF MATERIAL

Any training materials furnished to the Agency and to the Students shall become the property of the Agency to be used for training purposes only. The Contractor shall retain all its proprietary ownership rights in the training materials including copyrights, trademarks, and any trade secrets therein. The Agency shall have no additional rights therein except as may be agreed to in writing by the Contractor.

Figure 8-2.

5.1   SELECTED QUESTIONS AND ANSWERS FROM THE VENDOR'S CONFERENCE

Q.   Are trainers' travel expenses reimbursable?

A.   No.

Q.   Will contractors be compensated for the time spent in installation of software?

A.   No. Installation of software is considered a part of course preparation. Contractors will only be compensated for direct contact hours with the course participants.

Q.   Can individual trainers apply for certification on their own and as subcontractors or employees of a training company?

A.   No. Trainers must apply as either individulas, i.e., submit their own proposal, or as employees of a company, i.e., be included as a part of a company's proposal.

Q.   Is subcontracting allowed?

A.   No, except when a Teaching Assistant is approved by the manager for computer training.

Q.   What if I cannot attend my seminars?

A.   It will be your responsiblity to substitute another qualified seminar leader. If this is not possible, you must notify the seminar executive director within 10 days of your absence.

Figure 8-2 *(Continued)*.

their consulting needs. Should you decide you would like to work with your local, state, or federal government, write and ask the department of interest to place you on their mailing list. Complete all the necessary paperwork and return it on time.

SOME CONTRACTING MEETINGS ARE INFORMAL

Henry is a consultant for many clients in the federal government. He learned that a certain manager with the Housing Department was having a problem. Henry called the manager and told him that he would be in the building on other business the following week and asked if he could stop by and say hello. The manager agreed, and Henry got a chance to speak with him. He asked about the problem the manager was having with issuing purchase orders with the contractor hired by the department. The problem was discussed fully, Henry gave some ideas for a possible solution, and the manager was so impressed that he asked for a short proposal on the problem. Henry did so and obtained the assignment. Sometimes opportunities present themselves and make it possible to obtain assignments without the formal contracting meeting.

DEVELOP YOUR KNOCKOUT PROPOSAL NOW

In my experience in consulting and in the consensus of others in the field, to get the client to hire you will require that your proposal be a knockout. What does a knockout proposal mean? As discussed earlier, it means customizing your proposal with your potential client's needs or problem. You know your client fully before you put your proposal together. You plan your presentation fully so you piece together your written proposal with your oral presentation. Your presentation will stand out over your competition, and you will deliver the knockout proposal showing your client that you understand and will accomplish the assignment with your hard-hitting proposal, pricing schedule, statement of work, resume, list of references, awards and patents, publications, and other relevant information. All of these tools are discussed in the following pages of the chapter.

A PROPOSAL OPENS THE DOOR

Your proposal is usually a written document stating what services and benefits you can offer the client. It is an important tool to help you secure the assignment. The proposal should be single spaced to give it a professional look, and it should have large margins and areas of white space to help the reader make notes while reading. The proposal summarizes the information you have researched or developed from your meetings, telephone calls, and discussions with other employees of the company or others directly and indirectly involved with the client.

Your presentation should have a beginning, a middle, and an end. It should be long enough to show you have a focus on the situation and can key on the problem at hand. When you cannot determine the problem, keep working until you find it and then write your proposal. Many specialized consultants lose assignments or perform poorly because they misinterpret the problem. Spend the time necessary conducting your research on the problem to produce the best possible proposal. Remember that you are not required to solve the problem in the proposal, but you offer information about the problem and show what benefits you can offer to solve it for the client. Charlie is a government contracting consultant based in Maryland, and after spending many years in the consulting field, he still uses his proposals as sales presentations. He stresses the benefits because people buy benefits.

The proposal is your opportunity to show the client you are involved in the assignment and can make the contribution necessary to complete it successfully. Proposals help you communicate with your client. As a consultant, you are selling an intangible product, which is your ability to solve a problem or help your client understand an important subject. The proposal can be a documented record for your use as well as your client's. It will help refresh your memory of the problem or the issues you are facing. Proposals help you get back on track with the assignment as changes are made. Mary Jane is a financial consultant based outside of Chicago. She uses proposals in all her assignments, even when the client does not require one. When small assignments are requested, such as writing a small report or running a seminar, Mary Jane will write a proposal for it so that all parties understand what will happen. It clears up all misunderstandings and shows who is given responsibilities, including the times and places, so there are no mistakes.

PROPOSALS HELP YOU AVOID GIVING FREE ADVICE WITHOUT THE PROPER KNOWLEDGE

You are attending a luncheon of business owners in your area. Paul owns a television and musical instruments store which includes servicing. He learns from another guest at the meeting that your consulting specialty is helping businesses control and recover their accounts receivables. Paul asks, "How do I go about increasing our accounts receivable turnover?" You could try to answer this in general terms to stay on his good side, but without the proper research into his particular situation, your advice might fall short. It's better to say, "Paul, thanks for that question, but I would like to know more about you, your company, and the accounts receivable situation before I could answer it. Could I send you a proposal letter on our services?"

Notice what happened here. Paul wanted you to solve his problem right in the middle of the business luncheon. You could not do justice to him or yourself. By offering to do a proposal, you start the selling process. Now you have an opportunity to make contact with him for information before putting the customized proposal together. By producing a proposal, you are showing the client or potential client that you are a professional and you charge for your services. It also shows that you want to take control of the client-consultant relationship.

WHAT ARE THE BASIC INFORMATION TOOLS FOR THE CONTRACTING MEETING?

Your information tools such as your resume and your proposal are all selling tools because the potential client will review them fully before you get the call to attend the contracting meeting. Use the AIDA approach. Present your information to get *attention* and follow it up with *interest, desire,* and then *action* to be awarded the job as consultant of record. For example, Nicole, the audio and visual consultant from Pennsylvania, offers her services to many businesses and universities in the Philadelphia area. She shows her clients how to put together presentation rooms and theaters filled with the latest video and audio equipment. Before going to a contracting meeting, Nicole puts together a program that she calls "Proposal Basics" which is shown in this list.

1. Proposal
2. Pricing
3. Statement of work
4. Resume
5. List of references
6. Awards or patents
7. Publications
8. Other relevant information

THE BEGINNING OF YOUR PROPOSAL STARTS THINGS OFF

Get attention from your potential client by giving a background of the company, organization, or individual, if a sole owner, to show your familiarity with key information. This should include the name, address, how long in business, types of products or services, number of employees, sales, expenses, profit and loss figures, if available, and other information on officers and management to show your awareness of the assignment.

Let's say you are a consultant in negotiation and collection of accounts for various small businesses, and you're asked by a potential client to put together a proposal so they can consider your services to help them recover their cash flow. Here is a possible beginning for the proposal.

Beginning of Proposal

The Ames Company is a growing medical equipment company which started in 1991 and has doubled its sales each year for the last 4 years. Since it sells to hospitals and dealers, it has experienced shortfalls in its accounts receivable turnovers. This lack of turnover is costly because their line of credit with the bank is at the maximum and their interest rate is 14 percent annually. Their over-90-day accounts are almost 20 percent of the total receivable account. Their over-60 accounts are 15 percent on their total receivables owed. This situation must be addressed quickly to obtain the cash flow to run the business and contribute to the growth necessary to compete in this marketplace. Our consulting firm has the experience, skills, and techniques which can turn this financial situation around and put into place the right personnel and systems to keep the accounts within the normal 30-day terms.

Notice what happened here. A strong beginning in your proposal is assured by getting to the problem situation and detailing how many accounts are in the 90- and 60-day columns. You showed control of the situation by focusing on how your experience and skills would be essential to successfully deal with this situation.

MIDDLE OF PROPOSAL. The middle of the proposal is where you can focus on the key benefits your services will provide to the client. The benefits might include how long you have been in the business and whether you have successfully helped other clients in similar situations. It might be the specialized software you have to help recover the accounts receivable without losing the customer or it might be specialized information available to you that might assist your client. Never hold the benefits of your services back and secretly hope that your potential client will uncover them. Give this information to improve your chances of becoming the consultant of record for this assignment. You will not succeed as the consultant of record unless you detail benefit after benefit to maximize your chances of landing the assignment. Here is an example of a middle of the proposal in which you show how the client can benefit from your services.

Middle of Proposal

We can determine why a customer is not paying the Ames Company on time. Our consulting company does not want you to lose your customer or your money. To do this will require more information, so we have developed a unique system called the "Slow Paying Customer Profile" which can assist in identifying potential problems with those customers who are uncharacteristically slow in paying you. Once a full investigation of a sample of these customers is developed, we will be able to analyze the reasons why your company is experiencing these financial situations. Our services can help you keep those valuable customers you spend many dollars to attain and recover the money due to you. We promise to work as a partnership to protect your interests and work hard on your behalf.

During this important middle proposal stage, you have the opportunity to show what distinguishes you from the competitors which will be pitching the client for the assignment. Carefully analyze why your background is special, and can help the client, and try to show that this assignment will be a full partnership between you and your client.

END OF PROPOSAL. The end of your proposal is an opportunity to wind up the key reasons for hiring your consulting services and in a very professional manner to ask for the order. This gives you the opportunity to finish with a strong sense of confidence that you can complete the work.

End of Proposal

I want to express my sincere thanks to the Ames Company for your time on the phone during the past few weeks and for inviting me to meet with you at our introductory meeting. You have an excellent company, and we feel strongly that our consulting services can help your financial condition by recovering those older accounts. I can start work on your account immediately. You can reach me at 505-888-9901 to discuss this offer in more detail. I look forward to hearing from you. My resume is also enclosed for you.

DECIDE HOW TO PRICE YOUR SERVICES

Your pricing philosophy is very important to your success in the consulting business. You want to establish a price that will compensate you for your services and at the same time give your clients utility or their money's worth as well. When the client fails to get what she or he feels is good value for your services, you will have a difficult time getting additional work out of that client. A question that is asked in the consultant's seminar is, "Should I give the lowest price possible to get some business in my new consultant business?"

The answer to this question is not a simple one. It must consider what you feel your services are worth and what value your client will receive in the consulting process. Some consultants try to charge the larger companies or organizations higher fees and then charge lower fees for start-up companies and smaller, less established organizations. Your top priority is to run a profitable business, and one of the most important contributions to your profits will be to bill your limited time fairly to all your clients, large or small, considering your work and your billing rates. Stay consistent with your rates because it shows that you value yourself and your services. I enjoy the comment by a seasoned home-based consultant discussing how to set and keep the best possible fees, "You must be the one and only person who puts the value into your fees. The more you value yourself, the more reliability you will put into your fees." This is a powerful statement because once you learn your field and value yourself you will set a fee and then stick with it.

Your time is limited. Many beginning consultants fail to review the calendar on their office wall which should remind them that they only have a limited number of days and hours for which they can bill their clients. There are only 365 days each year, and discounting the weekends, the average of 12 holidays each year, and 2 weeks' vacation, you will have only 235 days billable to your clients. See the following analysis.

Total days per year	365
Less:	
Weekends	−104
Holidays	−12
Vacation days	−10
Total billable days	239

You will find that you will not even be able to bill 239 days because the early days of your business will require that you engage in numerous marketing and public relations activities in order to gather the new business necessary to succeed. You will find yourself spending at least 25 percent of your time in these new business-gathering activities, and this will reduce your billable time even more. Notice the change in your billable time once the marketing activities are considered.

Billable days	239
Less 25 percent marketing time	−60
New billable days	179

If you have 179 days for which you can bill your clients, you must be able to charge enough so that you can pay your expenses and still earn a profit. Remember that you are a consultant, a very valuable person to your clients and yourself, and you must be able to pay your expenses and make the profits that enable your business and your reputation to grow. Your billable days might only be 239, but the expenses to run your business will continue all 365 days each year. Your challenge will be to focus your energies and your sales forecast high enough to make your business profitable. A net profit is when your revenue is higher than your expenses. Let's say that with your 239 billable days you expect to be able to bill 10 hours each day, which assumes you will be working extra hours to gain this revenue, and you expect to charge $75 for each hour. This will be 200 hours per month, plus your other marketing and promotional work. Now look closely to the expenses that must be considered because without these business expenses you would not be able to perform your services. Review the following pro forma income statement showing the revenue from your fees and the expenses that must be paid.

Pro Forma Income Statement
Gilda Willmonty
Consultant

	MONTHLY	YEARLY
Revenue	12,000*	144,000
*(40 hours × 4 weeks × $75/hour fee)		
Expenses		
Telephone and Fax	350	4,200
Insurance	600	7,200
Advertising	800	9,600
Legal and Accounting	1,000	12,000
Computer	1,000	12,000
On-Line	500	6,000
Travel	800	9,600
Office Supplies	900	10,800
Office Equipment	700	8,400
Printing	400	4,800
Membership	650	7,800
Research	800	9,600
Subscription	1,000	12,000
Miscellaneous	800	9,600
Total Expenses	$10,300	$123,600
Net Profit	$ 1,700	$ 20,400

Your prices or fees must be high enough to cover your expenses and gain a profit to grow your business. The monthly figure for your expenses will be $10,300 and your yearly figure is $123,600. Your monthly profit will be $1,700 and your yearly profit will be $20,400. There are two ways to increase your profits: increase your revenue and keep expenses the same or decrease your expenses and keep your revenue the same. Get to know the revenue and expenses and set your fees; then stick to them to the end.

REVIEW THE STATEMENT OF WORK

This is your client's description of the work they want you to accomplish for them. It might be informal or formal. In most cases, it will be written and mailed or faxed to you. Other competitors will be pitching the client for the assignment. Carefully analyze why your background is special, why it can help the client, and try to show that this assignment will be a full partnership between you and your client.

This statement of work (also called the SOW) will include what needs to be done, the facts in the assignment including the symptoms of the situation, and why the client is requesting your services. For example, in the case of poor turnover of accounts receivables, it would show the shortfall of cash into the client's business. In a case where the client's problem is higher costs for their employees' health care benefits, it would show the increase during the last 12 months. What are the reasons the potential client needs your services? During the review of SOW, you avoid giving your analysis for the assignment or the answer to the problem. It should also include charts, graphs, drawings, outlines, and other factual information, including videos or computer disks to help you learn more about the assignment. Some SOWs are too detailed, whereas others are too brief. You might find that additional information is needed to make your presentation and proposal, and you will be required to call the client to get that information.

The SOW also includes some special considerations, such as the work must be completed by December 31, your proposal must be presented to the main office in New York, or the work must be completed for the sales meeting in Los Angeles and will be presented to the national sales force on June 15. Another part of the statement is the description of the final product: a yearly report, a detailed report, or a verbal presentation of your findings. The final part of the SOW is a schedule of key events, such as an introductory meeting, proposal date, or the final completion and delivery date.

Successful consultants know that a complete study of the SOW will help them make the best presentation possible to obtain the assignment. Sometimes, you will be uncertain about the reasons a client didn't choose you for an assignment, and the answer might appear in comparing the requests and information on the SOW and how you incorporated them into your proposal. One consultant in the medical care field solved the problem by making a checklist of all the various elements of the SOW and being certain that each one of them was included in the proposal before it was mailed or hand delivered to the client. You can do the same.

INCLUDE YOUR RESUME

Include your resume with your proposal package and make certain that it contains relevant experience and training which match the consulting assignment. Try to customize your resume to best present your most important advantages for selection as the consultant of record for the project. A sample resume is shown in Figure 8-3.

LIST YOUR REFERENCES

Some consultants will give their list of references on the request of the client. Once the client is serious enough about your proposal to talk with your references, he or she can call you and you can send your list. Be certain that you discuss with your clients that you would like to use them as a reference and get their approval to do so. Some clients become upset if you use them without their prior approval. Review the references regularly and request their continual approval to use their names. Your hard work and top performance will help keep your reference file filled with satisfied clients.

WILLIAM J. BOND

67 Melrose Avenue, Haverhill, MA   508 372-7957

Credit/Collection Consultant

Education	MAT DEGREE	— BUSINESS EDUCATION
	BS DEGREE	— BUSINESS EDUCATION
	AA DEGREE	— BUSINESS ADMINISTRATION

Many other post graduate courses, and seminars, and workshops, at American Management Assoc., and in-house collection, administrative, QLP courses. Developed my own seminars to train credit/collection.

Experience
October 1995 to present

Hardware collection manager, headed treasury teams dealing with customer requests, complaints, returns, adjustments, while doing dunning reports, preparation of cash focus reports, and other required company reports. I have also worked closely with QLP class, to bring QLP projects to RMO floor. Managed the charge call collection department, working closely with customers to collect non-covered charges.

October 1992 to Oct. 1995

Worked as a controller of a retail company, including handling the full set of books, setting up financing, doing related payroll, related tax returns for FICA, federal taxes, FUTA, and state unemployment taxes, and workman's compensation administration. The duties extended to hiring employees, full training and development, and setting full forecasts and evaluation of employees. My duties included setting policies, and doing a full identification of system needs, and doing monthly reports, and recommending and solving operational problems.

Teaching Experience

Professor of Business at Hesser College for 14 years. Developed career, home-based business, time, stress and priority seminars. Known for my inspirational, dynamic caring style.

Other awards and management skills

Winner of QLP idea for MQV Day in RMO, named hardware collector of month, September 1995, for collecting most dollars over forecast. Published author of books, articles, and works extremely well with clients. Excellent teamwork and people skills. Good time and stress management skills. Positive attitude.

Figure 8-3.

LIST YOUR AWARDS AND PATENTS

Let your potential client know about any award you have received at former jobs, association awards, and business groups awards which will help show your level of competence or involvement in your field. Keep this list updated to include current awards and patents.

LIST YOUR PUBLICATIONS

List all of your publications in the various magazines of your field, showing the date, name of the magazine, title of the article, and a summary of the contents. List as well any material you have authored or coauthored that has relevance to your assignment. Be certain to list any books, giving date of publication, publisher, and title along with an overview of the book.

LIST OTHER RELEVANT INFORMATION

At the end of the proposal, list any other relevant information, including hobbies, your cable television show, or your volunteer work with a homeless shelter or community program, which shows your interest outside your working field.

GET READY FOR THE PROPOSAL PRESENTATION

Read and reread all the various parts of your proposal package. Get to know the reasons you should be the consultant for this client. Review the benefits you will add to the assignment and to the client. Practice the presentation in front of your spouse, friend, or associate until you feel comfortable with it.

Before you finish your full presentation to your client in the contracting meeting, you want to finalize your discussion with the benefits you will bring to your client and to the work assignment. Review Chapter 2, where we discussed the benefits you would bring to the consulting job. Your client enjoys hearing about why he or she should hire you instead of others in the competition. Answer these questions: Have you worked in a similar consulting assignment? How did you perform in that setting? What working experiences have you had which will aid you in this assignment? How will your people skills help you? How will your analyzing skills help both you and the client? Answer the questions that the client will have within his or her own mind, the unspoken questions, to help the client make a decision in your favor. Never leave any relevant benefits out of the presentation, secretly hoping the client will somehow understand the unstated and select you. Getting the consulting assignment is hard work and requires selling your benefits. Remember to ask for the order at the end of the presentation: "Diane, can I start next Monday on this assignment?" You are starting to close by asking for the order. Now let's sum up.

SUMMARY

Learn the definition of a contracting meeting. Determine what information is needed for the meeting. Have the client give you pertinent information. The basic tools of the proposal include the proposal itself, statement of work, resume, references, awards and patents, your publications, and other relevant information. Practice your presentation fully. Discuss all the benefits you will offer the potential clients. Ask for the order.

Once you receive the order, we can discuss the consulting process.

YES OR NO: ACCEPTING THE CLIENT'S DECISION

Once you have finished your full presentation, you will begin the waiting game of getting ready for the client's decision. You have work to do for the other clients or marketing activities to attract new clients. Keep yourself busy on other work until you receive word about your presentation. Use this valuable waiting time in other important work. Also, if and when you are offered a consulting assignment, you will have to start thinking about preparing a suitable contract.

SOMETIMES THE ANSWER WILL BE NO ANSWER

In consulting, you spend many hours or days getting ready for the consulting process, and you spend days awaiting the decision as to whether or not you are selected for the consulting assignment. Perhaps they are not ready to make the decision right now, or they decide to keep the assignment within the organization. Hiring an outside consultant can be a very difficult decision for your client, and when all the proposals are presented, it makes the decision even more complicated. The result too often is a decision to delay or postpone the assignment of the contract. I enjoy the comment of a home-based computer software consultant about awaiting the decision from the client, "Whether I get the assignment or not, I learn more about my consulting practice with each proposal I present. Life and the consulting business take practice, practice, and practice." Your success will be the result of getting experience in your field and incorporating this into your proposals. Every experience can help you improve in your field, and this added self-confidence will help you land larger and larger assignments in the future. Just because the client decides to delay the decision does not mean your proposals or ideas are not what they expected or needed at this time. Avoid reading anything into the reasons the client decided to delay the decision. Put your energy and your positive attitude into the next consulting assignment.

WHAT HAPPENS WHEN YOU DON'T GET THE ASSIGNMENT?

You received a call from the client and she said, "Sorry, but we decided to offer the assignment to another consultant. Thank you very much for your time and interest in our organization." Let the potential client know you appreciate the call, and even though you can't work on this assignment, perhaps you could connect on a future job. Just because the door closed on you this time, by carefully working with the potential client, you might be able to use this experience to pave the way for work in the future.

Following are a variety of responses for when you receive a call, letter, e-mail, or fax stating that you were not selected for the assignment. The techniques you use to respond to the news will be an important tool to help you get future work or references from this client. Remember, you are not talking to a total stranger or just another potential client now. You have invested much time and effort in this company or organization. Use this special information and your contacts to pave the way for future assignments.

- "Oh, Roger, I'm sorry to hear that it went the other way. I felt my proposal was on track for your company. I thank you for all your help and for giving me the time to present my proposal. Perhaps in the future we can connect on another assignment."

- "Thanks for the call, Evelyn. I have learned a great deal about your organization during the past few weeks. Tell Diane in the importing department thanks for all her help. Please keep me in mind if other consulting assignments in international business arise. You have my business card and proposal should you need to reach me."

- "José, I appreciate your consideration of our consulting services. We enjoyed the opportunity to discuss your quality control training and seminars program. Even though we came up short this time, maybe we can work together in the future."

- "Beverly, I'm stunned. I was under the impression our proposal hit the mark for you and we would be working on the new sales plan together. Good luck to the winner. Please keep me on your mailing list for future proposals and bids."

- "Vanessa, thanks for getting back to us promptly. Just because we didn't get the work, we are not deterred and we want to be a partner with you on future projects. I plan to call you regularly to see how things are going with you."

- "Paul, I just got the fax on your selection of the consultant of record for the new computer system for your fine company. Thanks for giving me the extension of time to deliver the proposal. I look forward to pitching other assignments for you."

You can never predict the future. The potential client who turns you down today might want to hire you tomorrow if another assignment appears which meets your capabilities. The consultant who is selected might find excessive work volume and resign the assignment, and you might take it over. The potential client might recommend you to his or her friend or associate looking for a competent consultant, and when you show professional manners during a losing situation, your chances are better.

HOW DO YOU REACT WHEN YOU GET THE CONSULTING ASSIGNMENT?

You start off with a phone call thanking the client for choosing you for the assignment. If the client is not in, leave a message for him or her to get back to you. Tell the client that you are pleased with the trust he or she placed in you by selecting you and you alone. Follow up your telephone call with a written letter thanking the client and any other members of the organization who helped you put together the necessary information to win the assignment. In your letter, ask about what agreements or contracts are necessary to officially start the consulting assignment. Some clients will bind the agreement with you with a purchase order spelling out the specific consulting services. Just because you got the contract does not mean you can start working immediately without taking the time and effort to obtain a signed agreement of what you intend to do for the client.

WHAT SHOULD THE CONTRACT INCLUDE?

The contract should include specific information about the duties that all parties—the client and the consultant—are expected to perform. For example, Sandra, a freelance writing consultant for an advertising agency, started a writing assignment to complete an annual report for a large rental company. There was no written contract stating the duties of the client and Sandra, but during her contracting meeting, Sandra was told her flat pay would be $2000. She finished the job and 60 days after submitting the bill still had not been paid. Sandra called the client, only to be told that her work required excessive editing and rewriting, and they wanted to cut her $2000 bill to $1200. Many discussions went back and forth, and Sandra threatened to engage her attorney to get her money. All of these problems could have been avoided or minimized had Sandra set up a standard contract signed by both her and the client. Below you will find four basic principles to include in the consulting contract to avoid the hassles of oral agreements. Clients can forget, change position, or change the scope of their consulting arrangement over time, but with a contract you can keep the project on track.

CONTRACT ESSENTIALS

1. What is being provided?

2. When is it being provided? Due date?

3. What is the cost?

4. When is the payment date?

Fill in the information on each essential and include enough information to make your contract as complete as possible. Many consultants use their proposal as an important source of information to help complete the contract fully. Look at each new client in a new way. For example, let's assume that you are conducting a marketing survey on the present customers for a business selling software. What are the duties of the client to make the assignment successful? Will the client supply you with a full description of their products and services? Will the client provide a data base on their customers for you to use? How closely will the client work with you during the assignment? How often will you meet with the client? Clarify the duties fully and include this information in the contract. Some sample contracts are listed in Appendix C, Basic Contract Forms, at the end of the book.

How you are paid is important to you and your cash flow. Write your contract so you can get paid in the beginning, in the middle, and at the end of the assignment. Take advantage of the eagerness of your client to get you started by asking for and receiving a deposit at the beginning of the assignment. Here are several payment schedules you can use in your contracts.

Possible Payment Plans					
Deposit	10%	Deposit	30%	Deposit	50%
Halfway to completion	40%	Halfway to completion	30%		
End of assignment	50%	End of assignment	40%	End of assignment	50%
Total	100%		100%		100%

Discuss the payment schedule with your client before you write it into the contract to avoid it coming as a surprise. Your client might just assume that your pay will come at the end of your assignment. Sometimes the client will want to know why you are asking for your partial pay or fees in the beginning rather than waiting for it. Simply state, "The assignment will not be completed until 60 to 90 days and it will require costs on my side; therefore an advance of money is required." Stand your ground on your fees and your schedule of payment. If the client objects, you can decide whether or not to make an adjustment.

Once you complete the contract in written form and before sending it to the client, have your attorney review the contract to make certain you are covering all of your legal obligations. Once your attorney approves, you can then send it out to your client for his or her signature. Once the contract is at the client's office, expect a call to clarify something in it or perhaps a request to change the contract. You can make that decision. In the event the change is not going to produce a major difference, make the adjustment in order to get the consulting assignment started. If you feel it is a major change, discuss it with the client and see whether or not you can accommodate the change. For example, in a recent contract, the client wanted me to change the schedule of payments from a 20 percent deposit to 10 percent, and I made the change without delay. Be willing to work out the differences so you can do what is necessary to help your client succeed.

WHAT IF YOUR CLIENT PREFERS AN ORAL AGREEMENT?

In some cases the oral agreement will work, especially when you know the client very well, when there is a clear understanding of the work to be done, and when the work is a fairly straightforward assignment. But there is a real advantage to a written document that both you and your client can use in case of a misunderstanding in the client-consultant relationship. Tell your client that a written agreement can serve both parties well and stress the need for the written agreement. In the event the client refuses to pay you for your services and you have a written contract, this will stand up in court much better for you than the oral agreement. Time has a way of changing intentions, memories, and duties required by certain parties, and a written contract can help put things into the proper perspective for everybody concerned.

WHAT IF YOUR CLIENT REFUSES TO SIGN THE CONTRACT?

Talk to the client and find out why the delay in the contract signature. Expect the normal delay of the client sending it to his or her attorney before it is signed off. If you fail to receive it within 10 days after you have mailed or faxed it, call the client to determine the reason for delay. The successful consultant continues to communicate with the client during all steps in the process. When you fail to communicate and touch base regularly with the client, you lose momentum and will slow up the success of the project. Here are some ideas to speed up the process of signing the contract.

> "Don, I'm touching base with you to be certain you received our contract I mailed last week. Is everything okay on the contract? If it meets with your approval, I'd appreciate getting it back so I can get busy with this exciting project."

> "Maria, I haven't received the signed contract as of Wednesday. Did you drop it in the mail? Sometimes the postal service takes a few extra days, especially around the Christmas rush. If there is anything I can do, or to answer any questions on our contract, please let me know."

> "Sandra, I expected the contract returned this week. Did you receive it? If so, can I expect it soon? I'm really excited and proud to get started on this exciting project."

Notice that the contract is not *your* contract but rather is referred to as *our* contract. It will serve all parties. Diplomatically let the client know that the project will be started promptly once the contract is signed. Since the client is interested in starting and finishing the assignment, he or she will work hard to have it signed and sent back to you.

KEEP THE THIRD PARTIES IN MIND IN THE CONTRACT PROCESS

The delay in signing the contract might simply be because the client is so busy with other work that it slipped his or her mind. Another reason the contract might be delayed for signing is that a third party such as an attorney, architect, engineer, or insurance specialist is responsible for sending it out to the client. Check if an attorney or another third party needs to see the contract before the client will sign it. Try to learn the names and the roles of people around the client not only to get the contract signed but to gain information that will be important in helping you complete the assignment and future ones as well. You must also consider the key employees working with the client as important players to help you finish this consulting work successfully and on time. Communicate with the important people around the client from the beginning all the way through to the end of the process. If you find that the contract signature is being held up by the architect, and you know you will be working closely with this architect, call the architect and ask if there are questions you can answer on the contract to smooth the way to getting it signed. Use this call as an excellent way to build up your professional relationship and to help increase your chances for success.

BE WILLING TO NEGOTIATE AFTER THE CONTRACT IS SENT TO THE CLIENT

Once the client reviews the contract, and after relevant third parties or other employees have seen it, they might want to add more to the contract, shift the assignment deadline, or make some other changes. Your job will be to listen to their suggested changes and agree to the changes or not based on what is in your interests and the interests of the client. The agreement can serve both parties well, and you should stress the need for the written agreement. In the event the client wants to add substantially to the scope of your work, be certain that you can finish it within the deadline. Alternatively, you might want to extend the deadline to give yourself the time you need.

SUCCESSFUL CONTRACTS BENEFIT BOTH PARTIES

When you write a contract that is fair in price and performance for your client, your chances of being successful improve significantly. Some clients will read each word in the contract just to make certain everything looks okay; others will negotiate and discuss any sections of the contract that bother them. Work closely with these clients because they often can turn out to be excellent sources of work that pay well for your services. A consultant from Florida remarked about contracts, "I try to put myself in the client's place and ask if I would sign the contract myself before I send it out." The first contract with any client is the most difficult one. Once you complete an assignment to the satisfaction of the client, the next assignment and contract will be easier for both of you.

SHOULD YOU START WORK BEFORE THE CONTRACT IS SIGNED?

One of the popular questions at the consulting seminar is whether you should start work without the signed contract in hand. The answer is that it depends on the situation. If you know the client and expect the contract to arrive shortly, you can start the consulting work. On the other hand, when dealing with a new client that might offer some resistance, you might hold off the work until you have the contract in hand.

KEEP THE CONTRACT IN A SAFE PLACE

Once the signed contract is back to your office, sign it as long as no changes have been made and carefully keep it in a file cabinet. Send a copy to your client for his or her records. Occasionally, the client might make a change in your assignment and add additional work, and this must be added to the contract. Let's say you are doing a marketing survey on the sales of product A, and the client decides to add another survey on product B. Since the new work was given to you over the phone, write out a description of the new work and the fees agreed upon with the client and ask the client to sign it. Many consultants find it difficult to collect their money once the additional work is completed without the sign-off or a new purchase order issued by the client for the new work. Now let's sum up.

SUMMARY

Prepare yourself for the possibility of being turned down. Handle defeat gracefully; there may be other work for you with this client in the future. Keep the door open. Show your happiness when you get the job. Write a thank-you letter. Use a written agreement such as a contract to protect yourself and your client. Include the four essentials in your contract. Try to get some money up front by writing it into the contract. Try to be fair about changes in the contract, but protect yourself as well. Accept oral agreements if you have known the client for many years. When the client refuses to sign the contract, you must find out the reason for the delay. Third parties play a role with some clients; get to know them and work with them fully. Good contracts are fair and offer benefits to both sides. Keep the contract in a safe place. Get the signature on any additional work the client wants which is not included on the original contract.

Now let's discuss getting the consulting work done.

SETTING A STRATEGY FOR COMPLETING THE CLIENT'S WORK

Now that you have the signed contract or agreement, you can consider how to complete the assignment. Visualize in your mind what needs to be done now. This is the ideal time to utilize the information you have learned from the discussions with the client and from completing the proposal. Review the full assignment to deepen your understanding of your client, and this information will help you accomplish the work. There are four basic steps in completing your consulting assignment successfully, and these include: (1) planning the work, (2) setting your strategy, (3) taking the action steps, and (4) bringing it to completion. Putting the focus on the assignment and moving it along through these four steps will help you develop a reputation for finishing what you started. Become an assignment manager by performing all the steps necessary to start and finish the work.

STEP 1: PLANNING IS THE FOUNDATION OF THE WORK

What needs to be done to attain award-winning results? Planning means setting up a vision in your own mind of what you want to complete. I enjoy the quote of a successful human resources consultant who said, "I like to see the end results in my mind before I start the job." This is excellent advice because it gives you a challenge and an important goal to work hard to help your client. Planning means taking this assignment, which is really a sale you just received from your client, and managing your activities, resources, and special skills to finish it.

All businesses produce either a product or a service. In your consulting business, you are performing a service, but like any product which is successful, you must control the quality of the service just as much as the business owner producing a product. You must take ownership of the assignment by making it your number 1 priority to deliver the highest quality work to your client. Each quality assignment brings you closer to repeat business, and success in the consulting business requires repeat business. I recall the statement by Anna, a business consultant from New Jersey, "My lifetime priority is to become the best consultant in my field, and to get there I need to focus on the single assignment to build my business." Just as a brick house is built with one brick at a time, your consulting business is built on one satisfied client after another.

Planning is the mental process whereby you establish in your own mind how you will accomplish the work. The most challenging part of proper planning is to carve out the necessary time to get the work done. Planning means reviewing the time deadline. When is the assignment due? The assignment that is due next month will require as much planning as the assignment that is not due for 6 months. Carlo, a restaurant consultant in New York, plans his assignments into approval processes. When he gets an assignment to consult for a new restaurant, he breaks it down into three parts and finishes one part of the assignment and obtains an approval from the client; he then moves to the second part and obtains approval. In this way, Carlo is able to adjust his time management with his work assignment.

Planning means evaluating the assignment so you know it completely and can determine what is necessary to complete it successfully within your own time. The home-based consultant must plan one assignment at a time, and many times this means making arrangements with a husband, wife, significant other, or the children in order to spend the necessary time to finish the work. Sally had a consulting assignment and asked her children and husband to let her work on Saturday and Sunday mornings for the next few weeks in order to complete it. Sally has a full-time job and needs the weekends to help her establish her consulting business. As part of your planning process, include the people close to you when deciding what needs to be completed and how much time is necessary to complete it. Fred, who is starting his consulting business while working full time in the investment business, occasionally takes a vacation day from his job to complete an assignment for a client. A full day or a half day of total concentration on the assignment without phone calls, interruptions, and obstacles can make a difference. Remember that you are the owner of your time, skills, talents, and abilities. You must plan to use them fully in your business to succeed. Answer the following questions to help you plan each assignment better.

Planning Primer

	Yes	No
Do you have a full understanding of the consulting assignment?	____	____
Can you state the assignment in your own words?	____	____
Do you have the resources in place (e.g., data bases, computer, people, research sources, etc.) to complete this assignment?	____	____
Can you break the assignment into parts, such as part A, B, and C?	____	____
Is your home office set up to accommodate your assignment?	____	____
Is this assignment in your specialty area? If no, why not?	____	____
Are you willing to take full responsibility for your planning?	____	____
Did you include some rewards for yourself during the assignment to motivate yourself more?	____	____
Did you plan the extra time to compensate for unplanned obstacles and interruptions?	____	____
Do you have a friend or support network if you need some help or support?	____	____
Do you have an understanding of your strategy to complete the assignment?	____	____
Do you know what specific action items are necessary to complete the work?	____	____

Once you complete the planning process, review it fully to determine what specific areas will help you complete the assignment successfully and on time. Perhaps you can consolidate some steps to save time. Also focus on areas that may cause you some problems. Reviewing both the strong and weak areas will help you to deal with them when the time comes.

During the planning process, you will discover some important areas to consider. This is similar to the attorney planning to go to trial. The attorney will look at what important information is available and also consider how to deal with the opposition when obstacles and countercharges are developed by the other side. Your planning prepares you for what to expect in the future.

THE CONSULTING ASSIGNMENT CAN BE SIMILAR TO PROJECTS YOU PLANNED AND COMPLETED AT YOUR JOB

Sometimes the assignment resembles the work your supervisor assigns you on the job. The difference is in the role of the employee who, when faced with a question, can ask the supervisor or boss for the answer. As a consultant, you are expected to supply the answers to the questions because you are the specialist hired to handle the assignment. For the beginning consultant, this can cause some problems, especially when you place excessively demanding standards on yourself. The consulting business is a process, and it requires experience in all phases of the process to feel comfortable with clients and with yourself. When they first started in the business, the very top consultants of today felt the same fears that all people starting their own business feel. Nothing can take the place of experience in the field to enhance your self-confidence and your consulting skills. Struggling through and learning from the beginning of any process are essential to your progress, and with the proper planning you will be on the road to success. Christine is a specialist in helping small-business owners learn to use desktop publishing equipment. Her latest assignment is to help a small information firm train employees one on one and conduct workshops showing the various software packages available in the field. Since Christine never ran a workshop before, she became very nervous about it. After discussing it with a friend in the field, she decided to invite a few friends over and rehearse the workshop to build the confidence necessary to handle her assignment. Deal with your fears directly and, if the fear persists, consider seeing a mental health professional to help you deal with it.

STEP 2: SETTING YOUR STRATEGY

George is a safety consultant to various airlines and also works for many insurance companies. When George receives an assignment, it must be done within hours or days. There is no time to lose. To accomplish the assignment within the short time frame, George tries to reach the accident site as soon as possible and gather the evidence and data to present to his client. Sarah is a sales consultant who works with financial companies helping them increase their sales. Sarah's strategies include working with large companies, which comprise 70 to 80 percent of her business, and showing the sales force how to focus their selling activities to increase sales. José is a quality control specialist working with companies that need to streamline their operations and make them more profitable. José's strategies include training key managers and key employees on the quality improvement tools that can help the company. Notice how each consultant has an obligation to examine and choose the strategies that will work effectively to reach the desired result.

Focus on what needs to be done. Don't fall into the trap of trying to solve problems or develop strategies for work outside of your present assignment. For example, if you're hired to do a sales seminar for a software sales division, your exclusive attention is needed in this area. You were not given the assignment of selecting the best computer hardware or of showing them how to utilize the Internet. The other assignments might be offered to you later but right now you only have full ownership of your current assignment. Here are some strategies developed by veterans as well as new consultants.

Possible Strategies

- Interview the new engineers within the company working on product A100.
- Review the annual reports for the competitor of your client.
- Talk with key employees in the company to discuss their needs, problems, and suggestions.
- Evaluate the sales of the company and monitor the margins (gross profits) of each sale.
- Interview key customers of client A and determine their views on customer service, sales coordination, and communications.
- Survey former customers of client X and determine the reason or reasons they decided to stop being customers.
- Plan and deliver a seminar for customer service employees on time management for the Adams Company.
- Research the advertising campaigns competing with the McGann Company.
- Research other notable auditoriums before completing the drawing of the new auditorium for the client.
- Purchase and use client's products before writing copy for their catalog.
- Research all investment options for the client before doing a personal financial plan.
- Make a list of ideas to solve your problem. Write down every idea, even the silly ones, in your list.
- Interview the top sales executive to determine the factors in the sales slump of 10 percent for 2001.
- Show your client how to sell to the U.S. government.
- Write a letter to a major television show on the success of your client's new product.
- Spend a day with each sales representative to evaluate their sales presentations.
- Run a seminar with managers, supervisors, and associates to discuss and discover various communication tools.

- Evaluate the gross margins for the sales of the Access Company.

- Evaluate the hardware computer system to determine how it handles daily operations, including sales, purchases, order entry, cash in, and cash out.

- Do a full report showing how client P can sell its products using various sales methods. Include in the report how other companies in and out of the field are doing it.

- Do a full report on how the client can start her own cable show in her local area.

- Organize a focus group of children aged 5 to 11 to evaluate the toys offered by your client.

- Monitor the safety department's activities and determine whether the employees have disaster training for fires, explosions, floods, and hurricanes.

- Interview customers and gather data to help the client with valuable demographic information for future marketing.

- Research and determine the best target market for selling services or products in the year 2000.

- Work with a hospital client to find ways to offer profitable services while reducing or terminating nonprofitable services.

- Show your client how companies use creative purchase techniques to save money on their products and services. Include a report showing the savings.

- Investigate if client D can benefit by using a self-insurance program.

- Research whether a trade show booth can add sales and marketing leads, compared to present seminar programs.

Use these strategies as workable ideas to move your assignment from the planning stage to the strategy stage. Your strategy is a statement of your plan to complete the work. Avoid the temptation to choose some strategies that worked for you with client A but would not be feasible with client B. These areas might be addressed later, but focus on your specialty and the specific work assignment right now. Take full ownership of and responsibility for your current assignment. I enjoy the comment of Diana, a computer graphics consultant, who said, "When I talk about something I know very well I succeed; when I talk about or work on an unfamiliar subject my results go down." Stay with the strategies which will deliver the results you need to help your client succeed. Be willing to go back to your proposal and the planning primer discussed earlier in this chapter to clarify what needs to be done. Don't assume that you're on the right track. Continue to monitor your progress. Ask yourself whether or not your efforts are bringing you closer to the results your client will expect.

VISUALIZE YOURSELF FULFILLING YOUR STRATEGIES

Setting your strategies down on paper is an important beginning, but you must see yourself writing to make it happen. If you set a strategy to interview customers for your client, visualize yourself calling them. If you are writing a report for your client, see yourself obtaining the information and preparing the full report. See yourself starting those strategies, overcoming any obstacles, and finishing. See yourself presenting the results with the knowledge that these results came about by your carefully chosen and implemented strategies. See that satisfied, thankful client in your mind's eye. Ask yourself if you're doing what's most important to get closer to success. You know that the results will never happen without your attention to your strategies.

STEP 3: TAKING THE ACTION NECESSARY TO SUCCEED

This might be the most important part of being a successful consultant today. Successful consultants take action, whereas unsuccessful consultants just talk about it. Up to this stage, you have talked about what you want to do and you have put your plans on paper, but now you must take the required action to succeed.

Consultants that fail to take the required action are forced to make excuses for their late or poor results. People who succeed in business and life give results; others give excuses.

An example of taking the proper action is comparing two consultants, Jay, a public relations consultant, and Joseph, a financial planning consultant. Both have over ten years of experience in their fields, are in their late thirties, and have college degrees, but their working styles set them apart. Jay will only accept clients and assignments when he feels he can offer his best work. Jay sets a goal to finish the assignment by October 31st, and carefully plans his work schedule to meet the deadline. When Jay gets behind schedule, he tries to lighten up on new assignments and marketing activities to take action to get his assignment completed.

Joseph is an avid marketer, is continually sending out proposals and discussing them with clients, and sending e-mail to clients for new business. His current assignments were delayed, and often either cancelled or extended to a later date. Joseph expected to finish each assignment an hour before it was due. He is becoming a procrastinator and is hurting his business. Joseph must review his action programs or he might lose his business, while Jay's actions are building his business.

The business of consulting is much like this example. Your goal is to help complete an assignment for your client, and this requires regular action steps to finish it. You want to develop a reputation for getting things done, and this requires you to start the assignment. The first step in any assignment is to begin. By starting, you get a chance to see the early progress, and then you must keep it going to add to the progress. Action relates to time management. You might have all of the best intentions to take action, but your full-time job is taking the bulk of your time, or your present job requires extensive travel, or your family requires more of your time. Find the time to work the action stage of your assignment. Don't wait for a block of time to appear in order to start your action steps. Time will wait for no one. It must be used or you will lose it. Only you can be the time manager who combines action with the time available to get the results. Action is really hard work. Success comes before work only in the dictionary. Your assignment requires those small and large action items to bring it to completion. On the following list, fill in the action items you need to make a contribution to your work assignment. Keep your strategies in mind while completing this list.

ACTION ITEMS

- <u>Prepare the survey questions.</u>
- <u>Read publications on client's business.</u>
- _____
- _____
- _____
- _____

Take action on your strategy daily. Your strategy will not succeed unless you're willing to work on it every day. You can be successful in this business by using your time to get the work completed. Some consultants find that by putting that new work assignment on their to-do list it helps them to focus on their work and adds urgency to finishing the assignment. As you strive to complete one strategy after another, the assignment changes from being an idea on paper to a completed project. You are the manager and the director of this important process; you cannot delegate these responsibilities to others. Set the process into motion to get the results you need. Push yourself to start the strategy with one small effort at a time. Take the example of Ashley, a business production consultant, who received an assignment to write a report to increase the production of her client's service department. Ashley enjoys analyzing production data and math statistics, but dislikes writing. Even in school, she would always put off doing her writing assignment until the last minute. Ashley knew she needed to make an agreement with herself to complete the writing part of the assignment. She agreed that she would write a half page of the report each day. Ashley is a morning type person, so she decided to complete the writing early in the morning before going to her full-time job. You will find that each work assignment you accept will include various strategies for you to complete, and you can be creative in your efforts to complete them.

EXPECT FEARS AND NERVOUSNESS

Even when you work hard to get the assignment, once the responsibility is put squarely on your shoulders to complete it, nervousness can set in and sometimes slow you down. You're afraid that you cannot finish or that your work will not be accepted by the client. The fears and nervousness are normal, especially in the beginning of your consulting business. Think about the reasons you accepted the work in the first place. You felt your background, skills, and talents qualified you for the assignment. Now is the time to turn in the performance. You should know more about your work assignment than anyone else. Once you focus on a specialized work assignment, you became the authority on it. I enjoy the comment of Josephine, an educational consultant, discussing nervousness on a work assignment. "I like to think I know more about my work assignment, and the need to complete it, than anyone, and this keeps my nervousness to a minimum." Become an expert on your work assignment and the strategies and methods to complete it. Once you do this, not only will your nervousness and fears subside but you will begin to believe in yourself and look at yourself as the best in your field, even the best in the world in your specialty. I want to challenge you right here and now to become the very best worldwide in your field. You have all the skills, talents, abilities, and desire to be the best. I believe in you. You can do it. Just try.

DON'T BACK AWAY FROM YOUR RESPONSIBILITIES

Harry worked hard to win the assignment to review the financial and credit practices of his client, but he is falling behind his time plan for completion and now wants to call the client for an extension. When Harry analyzed his work style during the past few weeks, he found that he was putting new projects and selling activities ahead of his work assignment. Harry also found that excessive time, which could have been used on his assignment, was spent on sports and entertaining friends. For Harry to build his business and reputation, he must be willing to give the work assignment his full attention and make it his number 1 priority. By taking the responsibility and time, you will turn that number 1 priority into a success. Ask yourself each day if you are doing the most important thing right now to help yourself reach that number 1 priority. Here is a checklist to help you reach your priorities.

Your Checklist for Getting Things Done

____ Set a schedule each day for yourself.

____ You direct your activities.

____ Do your top priority quickly.

____ Get your work started and make it easier to complete it.

____ Reward yourself regularly.

____ Take short breaks often.

____ Do one thing at a time.

____ Don't spread yourself too thin.

____ Do things which will give you results.

____ Accept help from others.

____ Evaluate your progress regularly.

____ Look at things you do differently.

____ You are the expert in your work.

____ Get support from others.

____ Involve your client fully.

____ Ask questions to accomplish more.

____ Expect rejections and setbacks.

____ Keep telling yourself you can do it.

____ Use your evenings and weekends.

____ Evaluate time-wasters (e.g., excessive television) regularly.

____ Stick to your number 1 priority.

____ Avoid overworking.

____ Spend time with activities you enjoy.

____ See humor in your life.

____ Take relaxation breaks.

____ Believe in yourself.

Just as Harry analyzed his work during the past few months to find how much time he spent on specific work assignments, you have the obligation to become your own consultant and review how you are spending your most important resource: your time. Are you spending it in the most important areas that will bring you a return on your investment? Do you put things off which should be done today? Do you assume control of your activities or do you permit other people and things to do this for you? Be willing to manage yourself and your work.

STEP 4: BRINGING WORK TO COMPLETION

You will not get a favorable review from your client unless you finish your work. You will not obtain your fee until you finish your work and bring it to closure. Review your work regularly and determine whether there are things which need to be done immediately to bring it to closure. Perhaps you need to finish your research work or arrange a meeting with the client to obtain additional information. Allowing other people to withhold essential information will only delay completion of the assignment, and you will lose out. You cannot help your client until you finish the work.

EVALUATE YOUR WORK

This is an excellent time to evaluate your progress. What needs to be done to complete the assignment fully? Did you review your findings? Do you know the material sufficiently well so you can discuss it meaningfully with your client? Do you have an associate who could review it to give an outsider's opinion of your work? Remember that your client will be evaluating the work, so a thorough final evaluation can be helpful to you. Did it turn out the way you imagined it would at the beginning of the process? Why or why not? What have you learned about yourself in the assignment? Would you interact with the client more in the next assignment? Did you do enough research to get the best results? Keep a list of the information you learned from this assignment to use in future assignments.

Discover how this assignment prepares you for another one. As you bring the assignment to a close, think about what other possible assignment you could be offered by the client. You know the client better; you know more about the organization and what is needed to service them in the future. For example, if you did a marketing plan for the client, the next natural work assignment could be doing their annual report. If you just completed a seminar on time management for your client, the next assignment might be the same seminar using the Internet as a time resource or for a different department or another plant owned by your client. If your assignment was to set up computer hardware for the client, the next step might be to train the employees on how to use the computer equipment. Keep in mind that your presentation of findings to your client is an excellent time to indicate how your skills and talents can be used in the future. You must be your own marketing manager for your business, and the natural way to do this is to develop the habit of continually marketing yourself and your services.

CONSIDER WHETHER OR NOT YOU WILL IMPLEMENT THE FINDINGS IN THE ORGANIZATION

Your client might be so impressed with your results that you are asked to incorporate your findings into the organization. For example, let's say you just did a report on various ways for client A to improve profits, such as quality control, saving money on utilities, and other cost control practices. Now you can demonstrate how to do it. Give this some thought before you go to the client for the final report. Do you want to take the time to implement your findings? Would you prefer to do consulting work rather than implementation work? Will your time and work schedule allow it? Choose the work and activities which will make you happy. Focus on the work in which you can make the greatest contribution. When you enjoy your work, the quality will be better.

What Will Your Final Results Look Like?

This is a popular question at the consulting seminar. Just what form will the work take once you complete it and present it to the client? It will be typewritten or processed in two or four colors on a word processor or computer. Make enough copies for yourself and your client, and a few extra just in case the client invites some other associates or employees to the meeting. The report will be long enough to cover the scope of the work assignment and the findings or conclusions you found in the assignment. For example, Corrinne is a sales consultant for businesses, and recently she accepted a work assignment to find as many sales methods as possible to help her client increase sales and profits within the company. Here is her listing of 20 sales methods; her report also includes one or two pages on how the client could use the various sales methods in their company. For example, she details the third method, telemarketing, and how it could apply to their products and services and the thirteenth method on how referrals could be generated to help the company gain sales.

20 Sales Methods

1. Increase customer base.
2. Expand geographically.
3. Use telemarketing.
4. Catalog your services on the Internet.
5. Quote prices more often.
6. Add new market segments.
7. Add new applications.
8. Sell to Fortune 500.
9. Get to the prime buyers.
10. Listen harder (re: new policies, ideas).
11. Upgrade agents.

12. Support agents better.

13. Increase referrals.

14. Resell ex-customers.

15. Expand overseas.

16. Sell to the government.

17. Target showcase accounts.

18. Nurture existing accounts.

19. Measure and monitor marketing.

20. Define and stick with your strategy.

Include many ideas on how your findings will benefit your client. Remember that the report is for your client, and the more benefits it offers, the greater the chance it will be accepted and acted on. This will benefit you and increase your reputation in the field. Now let's sum up.

SUMMARY

Planning is crucial to your successful work. Review your planning primer. Set your strategy carefully. Act on it. Review the strategies given for ideas. Take action to get it done. Do something each day on your assignment. Expect fears; they come with the territory. Finish what you started. Evaluate fully to bring closure. Keep marketing. Decide if implementation is for you. Put your work in a professional package and sell it fully.

Now let's talk about the meeting with your client to discuss your findings.

PRESENTING YOUR FINDINGS TO YOUR CLIENT

Your work is over. You feel both proud and frightened about it. Your first inclination is to mail the report to your client or send it overnight and be finished with it. But you must sell yourself on the value of the assignment and then sell the client on the value of it as well. The findings are not enough by themselves. You must add that special dimension of your experience and knowledge gathered from the assignment. Your client wants to hear from you about how the findings can benefit the company or organization. Thus, your presentation will be client oriented and filled with new information. Or you will present a new way to look at an aspect of their business or their lives with motivation to do things differently in the future. With your presentation, you get a chance to help your client understand more about your work, not just an opportunity to read the report. No questions will be left unanswered. With a dynamic presentation, you can turn your client into someone who will be one of your most important supporters.

A PRESENTATION IS REALLY A SPEECH IN WHICH YOU DELIVER IMPORTANT INFORMATION

You hope you will be received well by your client and used in the future. This communication process is much more difficult to accomplish than to simply speak about it. A good speech must be planned and armed with solid main points based on your assignment. It needs to have a strong theme and move clearly from the beginning, to the middle, and follow through with a convincing conclusion. Norman Vincent Peale, the foremost positive thinker in America, was asked what makes a good speech. He replied, "Get excited about it, make it interesting, and keep it short." This is excellent advice for you in the consulting business.

Speak directly to the audience. By knowing the audience and making them a part of your work, you can present your findings in a way that commands their attention. What makes your assignment unique? What are the key facts or ideas developed in your work that will help your client? You might also use other work or life experiences, which will help you add an interesting twist to your presentation. A consultant specializing in marketing for businesses uses stories of other clients and how changes in their marketing methods helped them reach more customers.

Once you get their attention, you must strive to gain their interest by showing and telling them about your work and its value to their organization. This might be the most important part of your talk because here you can make the major points to sell yourself and your work to your client. Strike on the emotional motives of your client. Your client wants to succeed at work, to beat the competition, to be respected by others, to feel a sense of belonging, and to become financially secure. Your client is purchasing your services because you can help them reach these important emotional motives. Tell your client how your work can help them in the future.

The next stage is the desire stage, when you show how easy it is for the client to take the information and use it in the organization and in life. You are really saying that your results can work for them. You are bringing your findings into their world. Your success in your presentation is when your client believes what you say because they trust you and your findings. Nothing happens in your business or in your professional life unless there is a sense of trust between you and your client. This trust will be the cement which will keep your relationship with your client growing stronger and stronger in the future.

The final stage of your speech will be to ask the client to take action on your assignment and findings. For example, if your assignment was on a new computer system, tell the client what needs to be done next to purchase and set up the computer system. Make it easy for the client to get it started successfully. Show your willingness to support your client fully.

YOUR PRESENTATION SHOULD ESTABLISH YOUR CREDIBILITY

The presentation is an excellent time to tell the client how you followed through with your promises. This will show your client that you are credible. Credibility is the essential element to build your consulting practice, and without it, your progress will be slowed to the minimum. You establish credibility by being honest with your client, keeping your word or promises, and delivering your work on time. Credibility means keeping your client's work confidential, and you will only show the information on your report to others with your client's permission.

In your presentation, tell your client about the highlights and successes. Gloss over the slight setbacks and failures you encountered in doing the research. For example, if you ran out of time in your work assignment and could not interview all the managers in the XYZ Company, state that, but focus on the 35 managers you did get to interview. Remember that your client already has a copy of your original proposal and will have a copy of your final report at the end of your presentation. Your client will compare the two documents. Your talk will be an excellent time to clarify why the proposal may differ from the final report. Your presentation ties your research and knowledge of the assignment together for your client.

Speak about your assignment. Go over your report and focus on the most important points or facts which the client needs to know. Some consultants practice their speech with friends or other consultants before meeting with the client. After they complete the practice speech, they ask their friends to indicate the most important points in the speech, and then they compare them with the most important points they want to deliver. Since you are a specialist in your field and just completed this assignment, you are in a very beneficial position to share your information with the client. Discuss the things you know well and avoid getting into areas outside of your specialty. Practice your speech at home, while in your car, using a tape recorder, or using a video. You can make it better. An excellent speech will not just happen; it will take time and practice to make it just right.

Jack is an inventor, and his consulting specialty is helping other inventors or business owners market their new products. Jack's speech includes the problem and then the solutions. He then opens up the floor to questions. Jack prepares for the question-and-answer session by anticipating and making a list of various questions which could be asked and by writing out the answers to them. Corrine writes out her speech and includes a beginning, middle, and conclusion. She gives her client a chance to ask questions as well.

KNOW YOUR AUDIENCE

Get to know who will be attending your presentation. Will they be sales representatives, engineers, financial people, personnel executives, computer professionals, or a small group that includes your client and her assistant? Each audience has specific needs, and your job will be to show that their needs are being considered in your presentation. For example, if your assignment is about ways for your client to cut costs within the organization, your presentation should clearly address this area. Just as your work assignment must be client oriented, your presentation must be oriented toward client needs.

KEEP A RECORD OF YOUR PRESENTATION

Find out the official time you have allotted for your presentation. What is happening at your client's office on the day you make your presentation? Are you sandwiched between other meetings? Or is your presentation such a high priority that most of the day will be devoted to it? By planning your presentation in relation to your time frame and in the context of what is expected of you, you will receive maximum exposure and publicity from it. By doing a presentation that works, you have a better chance for more work from your client, and you can also ask your client for a letter of recommendation for selling your services to other clients in the future. Beginning consultants with strong referrals have an advantage of getting future business. Your client will enjoy reading your report and will remember vividly the enthusiasm and excitement long after the presentation. Your job will be to make your client look good. If you have been working with Alicia or Nick as your contact with client A, your excellent presentation will make them look good. Here are some presentation basics that you must consider answering to be totally prepared for your presentation.

Presentation Basics

Assignment topic _____

Presentation topic _____

Date and time of presentation _____

Time frame _____

Start time _____ End time _____

Speaker before you _____

Speaker after you _____

Size of the audience _____

People in the audience _____

What is the theme of the day, engagement, or meeting? _____

_____

Any sensitive issues to avoid? _____

Do you foresee any problems? _____

CONNECT DIRECTLY WITH YOUR AUDIENCE

The more you know about your audience from their jobs, their responsibilities, their artwork, their income, their educational background, and their goals and objectives, the easier it will be to succeed in your presentation. When you know your assignment fully and then consider the audience fully, it will be easier to customize your presentation for them. Show your client that you took the time and effort to examine their organization thoroughly. Make your presentation fit into your client's world. Your client will appreciate your efforts.

WHAT ARE SOME WAYS TO REACH YOUR CLIENT DIRECTLY?

Show how your research and your results can benefit the client. How can the client save money with your findings? How will the client's customers benefit from your findings? Tell your client you appreciated their help to complete the assignment. Stephen, a consultant on geology, makes it a point to thank the key people from the client's organization during the presentation. For example, he might say, "I want to thank Diane for her help with the graphs and charts and drawings which really helped me complete this assignment. Also Jim was very helpful to me by getting the financial information which was essential to this assignment."

Show the client how your findings relate to the statement of work. Show how you followed the assignment right to the end. Challenge your client to take the findings and turn them into the maximum benefits. Use visual equipment, such as an overhead projector, a video, or other methods, to teach the client by visualization. Tell your client what needs to be done to implement your findings. Show your client how to do it. Show your client how other clients have used your findings. Give a case study and other examples that you have personal knowledge of from both your consulting experience and your professional and life experiences. Speak the language of your client.

YOU BENEFIT BY EVERY PRESENTATION

Your first presentation will be the most difficult, but as you add the experience of each presentation, your level of confidence will grow and you will learn the elements which are necessary to make your presentation count. Dale, a financial consultant, made this comment on his first few presentations, "I was frightened stiff, but I kept practicing my talk over and over until I felt confident about it." You can practice your speech by reading it silently, then reading it out loud, and then by reciting it in front of a mirror. Then put it on your tape recorder or video, give the speech in your automobile while commuting, and practice in front of family members or friends. Practice is essential to your success.

GET FEEDBACK FROM YOUR PRESENTATION

After your presentation, speak with your audience on how they enjoyed and benefited from your talk. Did they feel you created interest in your presentation? Did they feel you displayed enthusiasm in your presentation? Did they feel you respected them? Did they learn the important facts of your assignment? Can they use the information in other projects in the future? Ask for any of their concerns or comments on your presentation. Review these reactions from your client and make the necessary changes in the areas which you feel can help you in the future.

USE GOOD PRESENTATION SKILLS FOR SUCCESS

Get to the client's office in plenty of time to make sure the lighting, overhead projector, and other equipment are in order. A good presentation will not just happen for you; it will be the result of hard work and practice. Wear your best business suit. Your best impression counts. Your voice should be loud enough so your client can hear you, but not too soft or too loud. Every speech is a free promotion for you to discuss your specialty. Top speakers are not born, but get better and better with each new speaking assignment. Look directly at your audience. Avoid the nervous habits of touching your chin, scratching yourself, or tapping the desk or lectern. Show a passion for your assignment and your specialized field. Talk from your heart. Use words both you and your client can understand. Read your audience. Are they paying attention to you? Are you involving them in the presentation? Are you listening to their questions or comments in the question-and-answer segment of your presentation? Use 3 × 5 inch cards if you feel you need them to help you complete the presentation. Tell your audience what you want to cover with them—for example, Part a, Part b, and the conclusion—and do it. Try to keep within your allotted time frame. A long speech can hurt you.

SUMMARY

Good presentations can build a favorable image for you. An excellent presentation is client oriented and shows the client how your findings can benefit them in the future. Your presentation must be well thought out and planned to make it work. Focus on the most important points in your report and present them in a dynamic way. You must know your audience and have an idea of what they expect from your presentation. You must connect to your audience by preparing well in advance. You must be willing to practice your speech before you deliver it. You will get better and better with each presentation. Practice good speech skills to succeed.

Now let's discuss marketing in the next chapter.

MARKETING YOUR CONSULTING SERVICES

Marketing is the process of systematically bringing your consulting skills to the client. It's the bridge that connects you with your client. In Boston, we have a bridge called the Massachusetts Avenue Bridge, which connects the city of Cambridge to Boston, and this is an excellent example of what you must do to succeed in your business. Direct your energies and resources to cross over to your clients. In consulting as in any other business, there will be substantial competition trying to use that bridge and reach the same client. Just as you must be creative in the way you plan your work assignment and look for the best possible results for your client, you must also be creative in the marketing plan you establish for yourself. Some consultants specialize in helping clients prepare marketing plans, but neglect to take the time to create their own marketing plan for the success of their own business. This chapter helps you review the services you offer and then develop a marketing plan to help you succeed. Marketing is not something you do a few months each year when business slows down; it is something you do each month of the year from January to December. It involves reviewing what you're doing daily for your clients, looking over your client's work-in-progress records, and reviewing your time sheets as discussed in Chapter 7. The services you provide are your products and your chief marketing job is to communicate this information to your current and potential clients.

KNOW YOUR CLIENTS COMPLETELY

Just as you needed to take the time to get to know your last client to get the work assignment and deliver the best possible results, your marketing success depends on your complete knowledge of your clients. It means asking some basic questions such as: Who are my present clients? What volume will they generate? How much will they grow in the future? How profitable will their business be in the future? Too often, many consultants are so busy servicing their clients that they neglect to learn which clients are their most profitable ones. All clients are important, but the clients paying you the largest amount of money should be given the attention and respect they deserve. For example, you might find that 20 percent of your clients account for 80 percent of your total fees or sales. You might also find that 50 to 60 percent of your clients are actually unprofitable, which means you are spending more time and expenses than you are earning in fees billed to them. In the following profit analysis, client L resulted in a loss because the costs exceeded the sales, whereas client P was profitable by $2900.

		Profit Analysis		
Sales (Billings)	Client L	$12,000	Client P	$15,000
Costs		13,500		12,100
Net Profit/Loss		<1,500> (Loss)		2,900 (Profit)

Does this mean that you drop all unprofitable clients and keep only the profitable ones? Not necessarily. It means that you must gather more information on the costs for the unprofitable clients. Why are you spending excessive time on certain clients but not others? Expect some swings in profitability for new clients; you need to spend time and effort to learn their needs, their organizations, and their basic culture. Once you learn more about your clients, you will be able to deliver better consulting services at lower costs. The key ingredient for marketing better services to your clients is information. Accept work assignments from clients that you feel have the potential to be profitable. Keep track of these growing clients and fill their needs better than your competitors. Take new accounts which fit into your long-term plan. For example, client F is doing only $20,000 in sales with you this year, but within 2 years you expect this to triple because your services will improve their operations, which in turn will help increase your sales as well.

Long-term relationships are built by knowing important information about your clients and then using this information to serve them better. For example, once Sandra, a consultant in New Jersey, started keeping financial information on her clients, she was able to offer the consulting services they needed. You should know if your client is making a profit or a loss. Your client will appreciate your interest, and you can operate your practice better when you know your clients better. Setting up a client data base is important, but it must be continually updated to keep your information current and relevant. Read your local, regional, and national newspapers, which report on businesses daily.

DEVELOP YOUR OWN MARKETING MIX

The marketing mix is comprised of the four basic strategies you develop to reach your clients. These include your product, pricing, promotion, and distribution strategies. These strategies combined become your offer to your target market. Your product strategy involves the services you are offering your client: research services, writing services, computer information services, surveying services, or seminar services. Does your service match a client's needs. Is this service relevant and up-to-date to compete in today's challenging marketplace? You control the strategies of your marketing mix, so be willing to change your service, add to it, or cut back on some of it. For example, many consultants in the computer area find that software services have been in demand during the last few years, and to stay competitive, these services can add to their sales. You are the marketing manager in your business; you must be willing to make the right decisions to position yourself to maximize your services to your clients.

THE NEXT STRATEGY IS THE PRICING STRATEGY

This is the price you charge hourly for your work or the flat total fee for a work assignment. To select the best possible price, you must consider your amount of expertise in your specialty field and what competition you have in your field and geographic area. Some consultants try to keep their pricing at the same amount as their competition; others charge more than the competition because they feel their experience and knowledge of the field warrant it. You may get a telephone call from a prospective client, and you will be asked, "What is your hourly charge for your consulting services?" You might be talking to a possible client who is shopping around for the best price, or perhaps it's a competitor trying to get pricing information from you. Rather than offer a set hourly rate over the phone without discussing the work assignment or the client's needs, ask for an opportunity to discuss the matter in more detail. Perhaps you can ask a few questions of the caller and determine what consulting is needed.

If you feel there is a possibility of working with this potential client, you might suggest an exploratory meeting where you can exchange more information about each other and uncover more details of the work assignment. This meeting is usually given free or for half of a normal hourly rate. If your rate is $100, you charge $50. In the exploratory meeting, avoid giving away too much information because you have not been hired yet. However, this meeting increases your contacts and gives you an opportunity to discuss your services. You are now in a much better position to get the assignment than if you had just given a set price per hour over the phone. Present your price when the time is right.

When you find an hourly rate that works for you and when clients are hiring you regularly and are continuing to do additional work with you, keep using the rate. Once a strategy in your marketing mix works, you must keep using it to maximize your sales. Be consistent with your pricing. For example, if you charge $100 per hour and you cut your price to $75 when a small-business client approaches you, you lose credibility. When you charge $125 per hour for the larger company, you lose credibility as well. By keeping your rate the same for all clients, you improve your chances of projecting your sales volume. You have only so many hours which you can work each week, so establish the best possible rate and keep it.

Ask yourself if you would purchase the consulting services if you were the customer or client. What are some of the considerations you would review before hiring a consultant? Your client will look beyond the price per hour and will consider your extended product or service. The extended product is really the solution offered: the findings in your report, the completion of a difficult task, the follow-up service after the work, and the security of knowing you're available to work in the future on other assignments. Your pricing must consider the client's buying behavior, and when your client feels your pricing offers enough value, they will purchase your services. Some consultants use an hourly fee and also a daily fee. For example, the hourly rate is $100 and the daily fee is $800. As the marketing manager in your business, you must be willing to make the right decisions to position yourself as attractively as possible to your clients. Some consultants charge for the traveling costs to the client's place of business, especially when it requires out of state or out of the country travel. This can be extremely expensive, so make certain that it is covered in your rates.

YOUR PRICING REFLECTS YOUR PHILOSOPHY

When you truly believe that your consulting work is important and relevant, have the courage to charge what is a reasonable rate so you can make a profit and grow your business. Remember that you are selling your time in this business, and you must get the best rate to survive. Once you develop a reputation and good credibility, it will be easier to ask for a higher rate which reflects your contribution to your client. The very best way to get the best hourly rate is to test various rates and determine which one garners the most sales for you. Review the following price testing analysis to help determine what hourly rate is best for your business.

HOURLY RATE TESTING ANALYSIS		
HOURLY RATE	SALES OFFERS	SALES
$ 80	15	4
$100	15	8
$120	15	3

Note that the best price will be $100 because you received the most sales (8) with this price. Remember that you must use various prices in 15 proposals for this to be a valid test of your pricing. You might find that the lowest hourly rate will give you the most sales because your clients will feel that the value received is more than the price, and this motivates them to purchase from you. Receive the best possible price for your work.

THE NEXT STRATEGY IS YOUR PROMOTION STRATEGY

This strategy means you decided on what promotional activities will work together to increase the revenues for your consulting business. Many consultants just assume that taking out some advertising in their local trade magazine or running some advertisements in their local newspapers will bring results. But simply running advertisements will not help you get the results you need in your business. It requires that you examine other possible promotional activities such as personal selling, direct mail, and other magazine advertising. Your promotional mix must complement your other marketing strategies. For example, if you are trying to reach small businesses in your geographic area to offer financial consulting services, you would design your promotional activities to reach this group. Once you find the promotional mix that works for you, keep using it until it stops being effective.

Take the example of Jaime, who is starting a consulting practice to help businesses sell their products on the Internet. The Internet has millions of users and is becoming an important market for numerous products and services. Jaime is focusing on selling his services personally and tries to get at least three or four appointments each week while he is still working his full-time job with a computer company. He likes to spend at least an hour with a potential client and customizes his presentation to show how his consulting services using the Internet can benefit the client. He is finding that some potential clients are quite familiar with the Internet, whereas others know very little about it. The personal selling activities must serve to educate all potential clients. Jaime is promoting his business by meeting with potential clients, sometimes over lunch, and going over his presentation on his Internet consulting services. After the presentation, Jaime must keep working until the potential client has enough information to make a final decision. Jaime found that to get clients to hire him he must make it easy for them to try a 3- to 6-month trial offer to use the Internet for their marketing services. The Internet market is huge, and in his presentation, Jaime informs clients that 35 percent of Internet users are women, the average age is 36, the average household income is over $75,000, and a large proportion are college educated. Jaime is presently working his consulting business part time but expects to be able to move into a full-time practice with the addition of new clients. Jaime's example is an important part of a successful promotional strategy to keep working until it pays off for you and to allow sufficient time to build your business with beginning clients.

Many consultants use a business card, a brochure, and some sales letters in the marketing process to obtain clients. Today, these are not enough for you to succeed in this competitive market. Your promotional strategy can be strengthened by setting up a planned flow of information to your clients. Your potential client will not read all the information you choose to send, so try to send the most relevant information to help them choose you as their consultant of record. Your business card should include your full name, specialty, telephone number, fax number should you have one, and your full address, so clients can mail you information. A business card might be the reason a potential client will call you weeks or months after you pass it out.

The brochure is an important sales and promotional tool for your business because it gives the client information about you and your services (see Figure 12-1). Take the time, effort, and money to make an attractive brochure to help build your business. This brochure will help you get new business, handle inquiries from interested parties, help you get appointments, provide important information, and close sales. The brochure should include your name, address, telephone number, fax number, specialty, names of satisfied clients, a list of your services, a list of the benefits your clients received from your services, your philosophy of business, and any awards or special distinctions you possess. Some consultants include their photograph, or a photo of their office or office building. For example, Sandra conducts seminars, and her

Improve Your Cash Flow

With 14 years experience as a Professor of Business at Hesser College, I can set you in the right direction to improve your cash flow with proven techniques for credit/collections. Attend this 1 day seminar and take home information that has taken most businesses years to develop.

Known for my inspirational, dynamic caring style, I have taught people how to setup their own home-based business, and offered many seminars on how to handle stress and priority management.

Winner of QLP idea for MQV Day in RMO, and named hardware collector of the month, September 1995 for collecting the most dollars over forecast. I will show you my secrets to success.

William J. Bond
67 Melrose Ave.
Haverhill, MA 01830

William J. Bond
Consultant

Credit/Collection Seminar

67 Melrose Ave.
Haverhill, MA 01830

(508) 372-7957

Front of Brochure

List of Businesses that have used our techniques...

Telephone Companies

Electric Companies

Automotive Industry

Wine & Spirits Companies

Major Department Stores

Fortune 500 Companies

What our Clients Have to Say About Us

"I came back to the office and immediately put into practice what I had learned. It worked like a charm. I could not have done it without your seminar."

Mary Thomas
Keystone Tire

"Wow! What a dynamic seminar. I really got more than I bargained for. I had increased collections so much from what I learned at your seminar that my boss gave me a raise."

Tom Peters
Ajax
Mechanicals

"I have already signed up for more of your seminars." The entire office staff has signed up as well. They couldn't believe the collections that I have been pulling in since attending your seminar. They are so anxious about attending your next seminar, I feel like I am a walking billboard for your seminars. I can't thank you enough. I looking forward to your other semi-nars with great anticipation. See you soon."

Adrian Miller
Millstone
Productions

Back of Brochure

Figure 12-1.   *Illustration of a Brochure.*

145

brochure features a photograph of her speaking before a large audience. Use a color other than white; sometimes a tan or yellow brochure can add to the impact on your potential audience. Make certain that you edit it and include all the important information to help you make the best possible impression on your client. Take out all unnecessary words so there is a smooth flow of information about your skills, talents, and abilities. Watch carefully for misspellings. Nothing can hurt your favorable impression more than carelessness. The best possible size for your brochure is the standard letter size, $8\frac{1}{2} \times 11$ inches, which will easily travel with a copy of your presentation or your letters to clients. Some consultants use two-color brochures to add more impact, but one-color brochures will also work. They can be printed by your local printer in print runs of 100, 500, or 1000. Once you have them printed, keep them readily available and use them to increase your marketing impact.

Keep a list of what you send to your client. You send an introductory letter to the ABC Company about your business support services. Later, you send an additional letter along with your brochure and your business card. Then there's the letter answering the client's questions, the letter requesting a presentation meeting, and the thank-you letter for the client's business. Keeping track of everything you send the client helps you promote your business better and avoids sending out duplicate or unneeded material.

USING PUBLICATION ADVERTISEMENTS CAN HELP YOUR BUSINESS

Advertising is an important part of your promotional activities, but since you are selling a selective service for a specific target market, your advertisements must have the goal of motivating potential clients to think about how you can help solve their problems. Some consultants use small space advertisements or classified ads to tell readers of the magazine or newspaper about their services.

Once you get an inquiry from the reader of your advertisement, you can then use the two-step marketing method, which means that you send your potential client a letter describing your services and include your brochure as well. I have used the two-step marketing method for many years in my mail order business: (1) receive inquiry and (2) follow up with information. This has proved to be an excellent way to build my list of possible customers. You develop this list from your inquiries, from recommendations from friends, from contacts in your field, and from telephone calls requesting information from you. This becomes your house list and it is one of the most valuable assets in your business because these clients or potential clients have shown an interest in your business by hiring you or thinking about hiring you in the future. You have an obligation to keep up the relationship with all of the people and organizations on your important house list. As you gather skills, talents, and abilities in the promotion strategies of your business, you will build this important house list into a list of hundreds, even thousands, of names, and each one is very important to your success. Guard your house list securely and avoid letting friends, competitors, or anyone else use this list for their own mailings. You can put your list on your computer to save time and effort when you do a mailing. Some consultants send out a newsletter to their house list to inform them of new changes in the specialized field, tell success stories for their clients, and include new services for the 21st century. Many of these newsletters are offered free of charge, and each issue can add to your client base. The newsletter is a public relations tool and will be discussed in a later chapter. It can be an excellent promotional tool as your own business grows.

Your promotional activities are so important that you must keep them constant. Successful consultants look at their promotional activities as daily occurrences, not just activities needed when a major client is lost or when business slows down during the snowy or cold winter season.

Your promotional activities must be planned and implemented all year long. At the beginning of the year, plan what you want to do for the spring, summer, fall, and winter. Think about how you can present yourself for each month of the year and develop a theme for the entire year. Is it the year of the computer? Is it the year of helping clients make more profits? Is it the year you can help your clients save more money? Is it the year you get more government business? Is it the year to help your clients take advantage of customer relations skills? Is it the year that you will show your clients how to use better human resource skills to increase their employees' efforts? Focusing on what you want for your clients makes it easier to plan a better yearly calendar. On the following list of the months of the year, note what you want to use for promotional activities. Remember that you are the marketing manager of your business, and you must use these promotional activities to develop and maintain your full marketing process.

YEARLY PROMOTIONAL IDEAS

January	Telemarketing
February	✔ Publication Advertising
March	
April	
May	
June	
July	
August	
September	
October	
November	
December	

THE NEXT STRATEGY IS THE DISTRIBUTION STRATEGY

This strategy is concerned with getting your services to the target market with the help of your best pricing and promotional activities. Your satisfied customers add to your sales. During the last few years, many companies have made strategic agreements with other companies to help them sell some of their products and services. These agreements are similar to hiring additional salespeople to help sell your services. Another important technique to add clients to your business is to focus on the important people in your field and the important people in the various organizations in which you expect to sell. Statistics show that 10 percent of the people in your specialty area can be important to help get your services noticed and acted upon for your success. Nothing helps your business more than favorable press and clients giving you valuable word-of-mouth advertising. William is a consultant specializing in helping employees improve their attitudes on the job. He received a favorable review of his recent manual, and a national newsletter offered their readers information on it and the address to get more detailed information. William received hundreds of letters on the manual and more on these promotional activities to contribute to the formation of his services. The distribution strategy is concerned with helping you reach out to your market, even when the market is worldwide. Remember that you have potential clients all over, many of them are trying to reach you, and once they know about you, the work can begin. Using the Internet might be an excellent way to distribute your services in the years and decades ahead.

NOW ALL OF THE STRATEGIES TOGETHER WILL BECOME YOUR POSITIONING TO YOUR CLIENTS

Expect that your marketing will take sufficient time to reach your clients and expect a delay before you see the marketing mix work. Your clients are very informed and difficult to please. Once you get the opportunity to serve them, work hard to keep their business. Good recommendations are earned from your hard work. The sum total of the strategies in your marketing mix will position you and your business in the market. This becomes your message to your market. When you make a contribution to your market, you will succeed. When you perform at the same level as the competition, it will take longer for you to succeed. Remember that the client is always asking: What do you offer me? Why should I hire you?

What are you able to do that my employees cannot do? In your marketing process, your goal will be to continually remind your clients why you are the best consultant. Gently keep reminding them that you offer important benefits which will help them in all your marketing activities.

Successful marketing means fine tuning your strategies to reach your clients. The way you position yourself is affected by three basic elements: your market, your services, and your own business. Your market is always changing, so you must adjust your services accordingly, and your business must make clients feel secure enough to let you handle the assignments and work for them. Figure 12-2 presents a diagram that shows the key elements of your positioning in your marketing. The key concept is that you might be positioning your consulting business to be the least expensive small-business consulting services in the area with the highest value received by the client. Your client will say, "Sally is the best possible consultant for the money. I'm glad I hired her." Now, through your hard work on the job and good marketing, your goal will be to have the client see you this way. Remember that the positioning in the client's eye is how he or she sees you, and success will result once the two positions meet. You have your work cut out for you.

MARKETING MEANS TAKING ADVANTAGE OF THE TIMES

Your specialty consulting field is always in the state of change, and to succeed in marketing means you must stay close to your customer. Joseph is a business technology consultant from New York, and his philosophy of marketing is to identify what the market needs and wants and then set a strategy to reach it. By contacting his referral groups, such as accountants, other consultants, and financial managers, Joseph is reaching his market. Joseph talks with his clients regularly to examine their needs and concerns, and he looks for trends in his business.

The consulting business improves during the bad times and becomes more difficult during the good times. It will be more diffi-

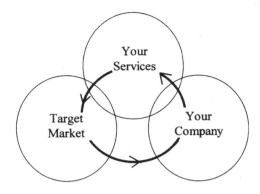

**Consulting Positioning
Elements**

Figure 12-2 *Consulting Positioning
Elements.*

cult to sell the business owner new ways to save costs and increase sales when she is making an excellent profit. When the economy slows down, many clients will be looking to purchase your products and services to improve their financial position. They need you. Your chief responsibility is to take advantage of all your time so you can maximize your efforts during the busy times and keep your marketing efforts during the slower times. One important skill I stress in my consulting seminars is to keep your marketing activities operating all year long, not just during the first part of the year or during your slow season. Laura is a customer relations consultant and she designs a month-by-month marketing plan and tries to use 20 percent, or one fifth, of her time in marketing activities to keep her business growing. To market your business, 20 percent of your business time means 8 hours each week or about an hour and a half each day. Just as you must keep your foot on the gas to keep your automobile moving, you must continually market your business. Now let's sum up.

SUMMARY

Your marketing is the bridge that connects you to your client. Your marketing success depends on your marketing mix, the strategies for your services, pricing, promotions, and distribution of your services. You need to know your client completely to market successfully. The sum total of your marketing mix is the way you position yourself. Give yourself sufficient time for your client to see you and your business in the same way. Your challenge is enormous. Your most important asset is your house list of clients and potential clients. Keep marketing all year long. Your market, your services, and your company affect how your business is positioned. Take advantage of the times.

Now let's discuss how public relations techniques can help your business.

MAKING YOUR PUBLIC RELATIONS WORK

When you see that consultant on the talk program discussing personal investing to millions of viewers from around the country, it was the result of someone doing some excellent public relations. When you listen to a consultant speak to your business or social group locally, and then see his or her photograph in the local newspaper, this is the result of public relations work. An article on a speaking appearance by a specialty consultant at a chamber of commerce meeting is shown in Figure 13-1. Public relations is one of the activities of marketing and should work together in conjunction with your marketing program to make a contribution to your consulting business. Public relations, unlike marketing or advertising which has a cost associated with it, is free, and when it is planned and operated all year long can be an important way to increase the awareness of your business and the benefits your services offer your clients. Public relations includes the activities by which you, the owner of your business or agency, attract the attention of newspapers, radio stations, magazines, and television stations to give the public favorable reviews of your services and products. Public relations educates the public about your business or organization. In short, public relations helps you get the word out to others, especially your target market or people who have an interest in your services.

WHAT MAKES PUBLIC RELATIONS WORK?

In one word: consistency. When you put together a plan which has a consistency about it and works with your marketing plan, you will succeed. Developing your public relations skills takes time, and the contacts you develop during your first year will help you in the second and third years. Your public relations program should grow with your self-confidence and the various experiences you

Creating a vision for your company's future

By TOM VARTABEDIAN

HAVERHILL — Drive performance. Motivate employees. Set direction. Continuously position your business. Establish a foundation for rapid response management.

These were some of the points driven home by Dr. Edward W. Deevy, author of the breakthrough book, "Creating a Resilient Organization: A Rapid Response Management Program," during a presentation sponsored by the Greater Haverhill Chamber of Commerce Dec. 19.

An enthusiastic crowd turned out at the Haverhill Country Club for another in a monthly series of Breakfast Club gatherings aimed at better business techniques.

And few know the market better than this authority.

Deevy is a managing partner of Deevy Gilligan International, a firm specializing in providing change management consultation to companies throughout North America and Europe.

An internationally respected expert on the human aspects of change, Deevy has presented his breakthrough ideas in workshops and speeches to thousands of executives and managers.

His book, published in 1995, became a runaway bestseller and a must-read for leaders who want their organizations to make it into the 21st century.

The management consultant focused his direction upon "creating a vision" and couldn't say enough about the work of Donald Ruhl and the Greater Haverhill Chamber of Commerce.

"He creates a vision for his community," Deevy said.

It's that vision that impacts people. Much of it was crucial in Haverhill's rank as the number 1 city in the Northeast by *Money* Magazine.

"Vision isn't the plaque on the wall," he continued. "It's shared by everyone."

According to Deevy, the success of any business isn't necessarily what goes on inside an organization as much as the external activity.

"The trouble with many businesses is how they think in an introverted way," he pointed out. "We must open up the arteries and share the information like solar energy. Success is your ability to respond to the needs of the environment."

Deevy was quick to confirm that one of the cherished cultural assumptions of traditional organizations is that business information belongs in executive suites and not on the factory floor.

"That's a big misconception," he said. "The real barrier is letting each player keep his own score. The goal is to create an organization that is flexible, agile, responsive and capable of surviving and thriving in a turbulent society."

His plan isn't necessarily paying for skills, nor is it in initiating bonus programs or profit sharing.

"The ultimate test lies in resiliency — the ability to adapt and conform to an unpredictable world," he noted. "Any pl[...] that places greater initiatives among th[...] work force will produce a net retu[...] above the dilution created."

Letting go of the past and keeping [...] with the times ranks high on his list of p[...] orities. Change is essential in molding [...] vibrant atmosphere.

"Frustration rises when people resi[...] change, even when it becomes necessar[...] for survival," Deevy maintained.

"Too many businesses and employe[...] become stuck in the comfort zones. Tho[...] who are constrained by old bureaucrat[...] principal need to undergo a process of li[...] eration."

Figure 13-1 *Creating a vision for your company's future.*

develop from your clients. Your public relations plan gets your message out to the people who are not hearing from you in your marketing plan. A business consultant from New Orleans writes articles to his trade magazine for excellent public relations exposure. Another consultant donates her consulting services free at her local chamber of commerce to help the chamber raise money for worthy local charities; she gets excellent public relations exposure. Just as the ocean is filled with waves moving to the shores each day, your goal will be to make your public relations program work so you get huge waves of publicity for yourself and your business. Good public relations means that you get exposure worth thousands, even hundreds of thousands, of dollars for free. It will require your understanding of yourself. Place yourself directly into the program.

HERE IS A PERSONAL CHALLENGE TO YOU

Successful consultants are competent people who make it an important part of their business to sell others on the reasons they should be hired by potential clients. Successful consultants know that educating the general public is essential to success. Keep telling others about yourself, and it will pay off. I challenge you to work hard during the next year to get your name and your activities into as many newspapers, magazines, and newsletters as possible. At the end of the year, you can post all those clippings and articles into one large picture frame similar to the example in Figure 13-2. You can hang it in your office, show it to friends, bring it with you to speaking engagements, and even add some of the clippings to your consulting brochure.

YOU ARE THE STAR PLAYER IN YOUR PUBLIC RELATIONS PROGRAM

Many consultants expect their public relations program to operate without their input and effort. You must make it happen. Your job will be to put your services under the sun. Let clients know about

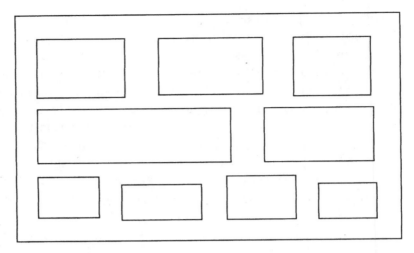

Figure 13-2   *Public Relations Activities.*

your success stories and the benefits you offer. It means giving your elevator speech on a regular basis and getting every opportunity to speak about what you do on a regular basis. It means thinking about your target market, what contributions you are making to it, and how you can reach other people looking for consulting help today to increase your sales.

Take the example of Diana, a career consultant from Minnesota, who helps primarily young people, recent high school graduates, and college graduates develop strategies and a career plan. Diana used advertisements in college and high school newspapers to reach her target market. She also works closely with teachers and guidance counselors to get client referrals, but she knows there are other unserved potential clients. Diana found that many thousands, even millions, of people were being laid off from large companies. Many of these recently unemployed people joined together and started their own networking organizations to help each other find jobs. Diana was asked to speak to their networking club meeting. She was interviewed for their monthly newsletter. Diana started to get more and more clients requesting her consulting services for help with starting a new career or new job in the same field. Diana tries to turn her clients into lifetime clients, who use her services for their whole working lives.

As the star of your public relations program, you must look beyond your target market. You have valuable skills. When you're excited about yourself and your business, this is communicated to everyone you come in contact with all day long. Whether you have a full-time job right now and are presently working your consulting business on a part-time basis is irrelevant; you are an entrepreneur and have important services to offer to others. Keep selling your services by getting the word out regularly and have a plan to make your efforts count. In this chapter, we discuss various public relations techniques and ideas that you can use to best present yourself to your specialty world.

USE A NEWS RELEASE TO GET FREE PUBLICITY

One of the most important techniques to share information on yourself and your business is to send out a news release to newspapers, magazines, radio and television stations, or any organization interested in your specialty. For example, let's say you just started your consulting business specializing in career planning and you want to inform the businesses in your area about your services. Write out a description of your business and the services you offer, along with your background and education in the field. You can put this into a news release, which is usually an $8\frac{1}{2} \times 11$ inch double-spaced sheet that includes news and facts for the intended audience (see Figure 13-3).

Your goal for every news release is to have it published. This requires you to have a hook on your release so that it is noticed and acted on by the newspapers or magazines. A hook is a timely story about how you started the business, how you happened to select your consulting specialty, or how or why the target market has grown over the last few years. Remember that you must impress the editor of the newspaper or magazine because you are competing with other businesspeople and other consultants trying to get free publicity. Show how this hook you have developed can help their readers.

You might also include a black and white photograph of yourself to add to the information in the news release. A photograph is worth a thousand words, and many readers might not notice your name and address, but will identify you by your photograph. Once you mail your news release, watch future issues of the newspaper

---

NEWS RELEASE

FROM: Sylvia Bloomberg   DATE: Feb. 8, 1999

            7 Buckingham Road, Groveland, MA 01834

PHONE: 508 888-4311

TO: The Winchester Star Newspaper

SUBJECT: New Consulting Business Opening

Sylvia M. Bloomberg recently opened a new consulting practice specializing in showing clients how to change and manage their careers more successfully.

Ms. Bloomberg has worked in human resources for the last 15 years with various service, computer, and advertising agencies. She is a graduate of Salem College with a BS degree in Education and holds a Master of Business Administration degree from Lesley College.

Ms. Bloomberg always wanted to help people with their careers. She said, "I'm excited to be able to use my skills and experience and help others grow in their jobs and careers." She will be offering a free 1-hour seminar entitled 'Career Planning" at the Haverhill Public Library on Monday evenings during the month of June.

Ms. Bloomberg's office will be at 7 Buckingham Road in Groveland and she can be reached at 508 888-4311. She will be happy to meet free with potential clients to describe her various career programs, from the 30 day career program to the full 2 year career management program.

Figure 13-3 *News Release.*

or magazine to see if your news release was selected. Do not call the editor to find out whether or not you were selected or to apply pressure to get your release published. Nothing makes editors more upset than people who hound them about their news stories. Make certain that you include your full name, address, and telephone number so the editor can call you with any questions.

Sometimes you send a news release and the editor likes it and your idea but puts it aside to use another time. Although it might actually be used later, there are times it will be set aside and forgotten. I have had cases when I called the editor and shared an idea for a news story on my business, and if the editor seemed receptive to it, I would ask, "Would you like to get together and talk about home-based businesses in the 21st century?" Once I get a positive answer from the editor, I set up a time and place immediately. I usually choose to go to the editor's office and bring along any information about my business activities which relate to the story. Do not bring news clippings of other articles about you and your business because the editor or writer might feel you have appeared too often and change his or her mind on the story. It would be better to take a brochure and some information on the services you are providing for your clients.

Try to talk about success stories you have accomplished for your clients. If you are asked a question and cannot answer it, avoid trying to answer it by giving the wrong information. Tell the writer that you are not sure, but you could find out the answer and get back as soon as possible. Once the interview is over, thank the writer, give your business card, and leave promptly. The writer may have deadlines, and wants to get back to the daily work. Write or call the writer to say thanks within a few days after the interview.

A free article about you and your business is worth thousands of dollars in advertising. Make copies of it once it is published for handouts to potential clients.

RADIO APPEARANCES CAN REACH A WIDE AUDIENCE

Thousands of people listen to the radio driving to work, while at work, and during the evenings and weekends. To determine what radio stations might be interested in hearing about your specialty, think about the stations you listen to while commuting to work and during your off-work hours. For example, there are radio shows on various topics such as sports, business, environment, home-based businesses, investments, health and diet, politics, entertainment, and many other subjects. Once you determine that you would like to appear on a specific show, take the time to note what topics and guests they have been booking for the show. In the beginning, try to select a local show in your area. The host of the show may or may not have any input on the selection of guests, and the decision could be made solely by the programming manager.

Find a hook in your specialty and how it could connect the listeners of the show. For example, if you are an investment consultant, you might want to present an appearance entitled "The Beginner's Personal Investment Program" on the show, whereby you discuss how to start an investment program. This topic shows that you are interested in helping listeners start their own investment program. Write a letter to the programming manager of the show of your choice. Include your business card, a brochure, or other information which relates to your qualifications to present your information. Follow up in a week or 10 days and ask to speak to the programming manager. Discuss your reasons for presenting the topic and the benefits it will bring to the audience. All radio and television shows are required by the Federal Communications Commission to present shows or programming that are in the interest of the public. Once you show your topic is in the public interest, your chances for an appearance increase substantially. If you are turned down the first time, avoid getting angry. Just accept it and keep trying again in the future.

Once you receive an acceptance from the show, set up a time and date that will give you an opportunity to prepare for the appearance. Schedule it at a time which avoids excessive travel to arrive at the station; you never want to be late for any appointment, and this is especially true of a radio or television show. Once you book for 2 P.M. on January 15, you must be certain to be there on that day and arrive 10 to 15 minutes ahead of time. To help you get responses from your appearance, try to give the listeners something for free. It might be an article you wrote on investments or a description of the various ways to invest their money, such as stocks, bonds, mutual funds, savings, and certificates of deposits. Ask the programming manager for permission to offer it during the show or at the end of the show. When you offer this free information, you get a chance to add names to your house mailing list, and you can turn these listeners into future clients. The people receiving your information will tell friends about you and give you valuable word-of-mouth advertising. I had this experience on a radio show recently. I offered a free article on home-based businesses to the listeners free of charge if they would send me a self-addressed, stamped envelope. A few days later, I received hundreds of responses so I simply placed the free article in the envelope along with a letter describing my services and my business card. This is an excellent way to gain excellent public relations, talk with various people on the radio, and add to your house mailing list.

Follow up with the people who requested the free information and see if you can answer any questions they might have for you. Perhaps you can set up an appointment to fully describe your services to them in person. Consider doing a free seminar locally for people who responded. Good marketing, selling, and public relations mean following up to keep the customer or potential client happy. A few days after the radio appearance, write a thank-you letter to both the radio host and the programming manager.

TELEVISION SHOWS CAN MAKE YOU A WELL-KNOWN CONSULTANT

Once you learn the skills necessary to obtain the print and radio publicity, you are ready to pursue the more complicated and competitive television publicity. Many consultants are trying to appear on television shows to reap the enormous benefits of connecting to thousands and millions of viewers, some of whom are potential clients or can recommend you to other friends, associates, and relatives. Television is the magic medium which has played an important role in building businesses for consultants in all fields.

Choose a show offering topics that relate to your specialty and write a letter to the programming manager describing your idea.

Think carefully about the hook for the show and the benefits viewers will receive from your appearance. Make certain you include your business card and a brochure of your services, and the programming manager can get a brochure back to you. If you fail to get a letter or call back from the show, phone to see whether or not they will take the time to see you about your possible appearance on the show. Be willing to mention that you have had experience appearing on the radio, and this will be an added benefit to you. Ask the programming manager if you have sent enough information to make a decision. If more material is needed, you can send articles, manuals, or books you have written and a list of any seminars you have presented. Some consultants send what is called a press kit, and this includes a resume, photograph, brochure, list of clients served, articles, manuals, and books. The press kit serves to get you noticed and selected to appear on radio and television shows and offers material for making a presentation for a work assignment.

Take the example of Florence, a specialist in helping laid off employees find other careers and jobs, who recently appeared on a television show offering advice for people recently laid off or threatened by a staff reduction at work. Florence did an excellent presentation on the show because she discussed her experience with various people in different age groups who related how they had coped with their new employment status. She showed how the newly laid off employee must deal with the mental side of the situation, and once that is addressed, take the action to find a new opportunity. Florence described the stages each person goes through before a strategy can be selected to move on to success. She even took questions from people in the audience, and answered them very well. Florence showed that once you know your specialty well enough, you can discuss it in a meaningful way not only with clients and potential clients but with the public as well.

I recommend that you deal with a local television station in the beginning, and as you develop more skills, you can move on to regional and network shows. Keep a list of all your contacts at each station and send thank-you notes to all the shows you appear on. The larger the show, the greater the response you will receive from the public, so be ready to handle the response accordingly.

SPONSOR A SPEAKER

You can get publicity by finding a speaker who has expertise in a specific area and will speak to your clients or potential clients about it. Avoid any speakers addressing topics in your consulting specialty. There are a number of local specialists in subjects such as medical insurance planning, small-business skills, software selection, using the Internet, tax saving ideas, how to land a job in the 21st century, and home-based business opportunities. Remember that people are interested in making money, saving money, attracting other people, improving their careers, and improving their diets. You can invite someone to speak to your business group or hire a hall for an evening and invite all the people who will enjoy the topic. Phone the potential speaker and ask him or her to appear at your meeting. Don't worry about being turned down; most people are flattered when asked to speak before the public. Here is a dialogue that might work for you.

> BETH: Hello, Susan. This is Beth Wellington. On Thursday evening February 12th, we are sponsoring an exciting evening to discuss business skills for small-business owners. One valuable skill is time management, and I know this is your specialty. Would you like to share some of your expertise and experience by addressing our group?
>
> SUSAN: Oh, thank you for the invitation, but I'm not sure I can make it. My schedule is full. How long do you expect the speech to be?
>
> BETH: I am very flexible on time. It should be at least 30 minutes up to 45 minutes maximum. Some of our speakers extend their time by having a question-and-answer session at the end of their presentation.
>
> SUSAN: Oh, that sounds good. I think I could put together a program similar to the one I use now. Can I hand out an article I wrote for a professional magazine on using time effectively?
>
> BETH: You certainly can. You will get excellent exposure. Can we book the date now and talk about the specifics later?
>
> SUSAN: Yes, let's book it.
>
> BETH: Thank you very much.

You are not required to pay the speaker. If the speaker asks about the fee for the speech, mention that no fee is given, but it will be excellent for public relations and free publicity. Also mention it will be covered by the local newspapers. Many speakers will accept the speaking assignment because they know the value of talking to different audiences about a subject they know very well. Once you book your speaker, make sure you send a news release to your local newspaper, trade magazine, or chamber of commerce publicity department. Inform them of your speaker and the benefits offered in the speech so that you will fill the hall. Nothing upsets the speaker more than a handful of people in a large hall after the speaker has prepared the speech, traveled to the hall, and looked forward to a large audience. Give yourself enough time to promote the meeting so you can get the maximum attendance. Give the speaker a small gift as a memento of the speech and send a thank-you letter after the speech.

As you gather experience in sponsoring speakers and in seeing and hearing them develop various topics, you will develop confidence in yourself as a potential speaker. Choose a topic which relates to your specialty and write out an outline of the topics to cover. Practice the speech in front of a mirror or into a tape recorder until you can deliver it just the way you want. Contact the business groups, service clubs such as the Kiwanis, Elks, Rotary, and Exchange, and various other clubs that offer weekly meetings and need speakers. Make sure you book only on dates when you are sure you will be able to show up on time. Nothing hurts a speaker's reputation more than arriving late or having to cancel because of schedule conflicts. Make certain you have a supply of business cards to hand out before and after your speech. Follow up later with the new contacts from the audience to communicate how your services can benefit them.

RUN YOUR OWN PUBLIC RELATIONS SEMINAR

A powerful publicity tool for your consulting business is showcasing your knowledge and skills to your clients, potential clients, and the general public at a seminar. There are two types of seminars: the public relations seminar and the seminar for profit. The public relations seminar is given to present material and information about your business to stimulate inquiries from people who attended your seminar or heard about you from the seminar. You might charge a small fee to attend but do not expect to generate a profit from the seminar itself. Its primary purpose is to increase sales leads for increased business. The seminars for profit, on the other hand, are carefully planned programs that usually last at least half a day. Most are a day in length, or even 2 days, and there is a cost for each applicant. You are conducting these seminars for profit. They form part of the profitable spin-offs, or additional products or services you can sell, to increase your business. The seminars for profit are discussed in greater detail in Chapter 16 in this book.

One of the best ways to put on your own public relations seminar is to choose a subject you know very well or even one which complements your present consulting specialty. For example, if your specialty is advertising on cable television, you could conduct a public relations seminar entitled "Seven Steps to Your Advertising on a Cable Television Program" and present it to local business owners.

The public relations seminar is usually 2 to 3 hours long. In many cases it is free or with a small charge, usually $25 to $50 for each applicant to defray the cost of hiring a hall and mailing out the invitations. Since the public relations seminar will take time and effort to make it a success, you want to invite only qualified people who have the desire and income to purchase your consulting services. Invite people who have inquired about your services in the past. Look over your house list. Some public relations seminars offer a number of specialists who form a panel, and each one discusses his or her specialty. They take questions at the end of the program. As a participant in the seminar, use the forum to show others that you are an expert in your fields and that you can benefit others with your specialized knowledge. Expect difficult questions and give them full answers. By holding back, the attendees of the seminars may feel you lack the knowledge. You may feel the attendees are just asking questions to get answers for the inexpensive price of your seminar, but by answering their questions completely, you will get more business. This exposure can showcase your expertise. When you set up your seminar, make certain that you have sufficient material to utilize every minute of the time allotted. If a 3-hour seminar is over in 2 hours, people will feel cheated no matter how much they have learned.

The seminar differs from the speech. You will be presenting more material and covering a topic in more detail, and you will be asked more questions by your attendees. Following are the various steps necessary to set up a successful public relations seminar. Remember that the goal of your seminar is to educate your attendees that you have what it takes to be a consultant for them in your specialized filed.

SUCCESS STEPS FOR YOUR PUBLIC RELATIONS SEMINAR

1. Select a relevant topic.
2. Tie it directly to your specialty.
3. Send out personal invitations.
4. Ask your attendees to preregister.
5. Present it during the normal workday, 9 A.M. to 12 P.M. or 1 P.M. to 4 P.M.
6. Keep the seminar on time to cover all the material.
7. Take time to answer questions fully.
8. Hold a get acquainted session at the end of the seminar to talk with your attendees.
9. Exchange business cards, brochures, and ideas at end.
10. Follow up with the attendees to set up work assignment appointments.

The payoffs for your public relations seminar will be the contacts you meet, but there are other important payoffs as well. Ask a friend to come to your seminar and shoot a video, including your full presentation on your specialty. You can give this video a title, such as "Investing in Top Mutual Funds," and sell it as a product in your business or send it to potential clients. If you cannot ask or pay a friend to take the video for you, consider hiring a video specialist. This will be another product you can sell to others in the future. You will be building your line of products and services. You can make a video during your speech to your local Women's Professional Club or the Kiwanis Club as long as you get their permission prior to appearing before their group. I recently spoke at a meeting in Massachusetts for a management accounting group and hired a video production specialist to develop a video of my performance at the meeting. I can now use this video for potential clients and also include it in my catalog with my articles, books, and manuals. You can do the same. Take every opportunity to turn public relations activities into potential products and services.

NOW YOU ARE READY TO TEACH A CLASS OR A COURSE

The experience you gather in delivering various speeches to local, regional, or trade groups will help you prepare and develop your own class or course in your specialized field. The difference between a class and a course is the length of time associated with it. If you teach a special interest class entitled "How to Purchase a Business" at the local community college or high school, you can run it for one evening session or up to 3 or 4 weeks. A course usually runs from 8 to 16 weeks and can be your own topic or a standard course regularly offered by the college or school. Examples of courses include business law, accounting, English, psychology, marketing, business management, real estate, child psychology, and many others. The closer your specialty relates to the class or course, the better. You will gain excellent public relations from it and gather presentation skills at the same time.

An attorney teaches a business law course at his local community college and will not accept a paycheck for his teaching. The college has presented him with special awards for this contribution, and he has had his photograph and a related story in the local newspaper. This free publicity is far more valuable to him than any advertising he could purchase, even if he paid thousands of dollars for it.

I recommend that you start off by teaching a special interest class and hand out materials in the class from publications you have written and other material to show your grasp of the field. Colleges and high schools are in the adult education business, and their specialty is to showcase local people who have specialized information to present to others. Write a letter to the director of the evening adult education department of your local community college or high school. Discuss the benefits your special interest class will offer to students and discuss your speaking experience and the experience you have developed in your consulting business. Do not give the impression on paper or in person that you are teaching primarily to develop contacts and potential clients. Include an outline of the material you plan to offer in your class and a copy of your resume. College degrees are not required to teach special interest classes, but may be required for a course.

Give the school or college about 2 weeks to get back to you. If you don't hear from them, call to see if they have received your material. Try to set up an interview with the director or person in charge of the hiring process. Dress like you are going to a contracting meeting with a client and show your excitement about your class, your specialty, and the benefits you have to offer. Review the material you mailed earlier and reinforce the important points it contains. Tell the director you are willing to add different classes in the future.

Many consultants find that the director will offer the class in the next catalog to the students and will run it when at least eight or ten students sign up. In my own experience, my first few classes did not pull, but when I presented a class entitled "Ten Best Home Businesses," the enrollment improved enormously. I had to run extra classes to handle the overload. The important point here is that it takes time for your first few classes to pull enough students to run them. But the experience you gather and the information you learn from your students will pay you tremendous returns. Your students will evaluate you at the end of your course or class. Read the evaluations over and develop insight into ways you might change to make your next class even better. I probably learned more in the special interest classes I taught than my students did. I learned that I could extend my classes in the form of writing articles and newsletters to my potential clients. My classes help me to expand my limited imagination of ways to reach and help my potential clients.

WRITE ABOUT YOUR SPECIALTY

To expand the potential market for your clients, you can use an important public relations tool: the written word. Many of your potential clients will read about you or read an article you have written in a newspaper or trade magazine.

You are not required to be a professional writer to learn to write articles of interest to your field or specialty. The most important rule is to write about a subject you know very well. Take every opportunity to write that is offered to you. Many consultants agree that the ability to write is a very valuable and rewarding skill. It requires patience and practice. I recommend that my consulting seminar attendees write letters to the editor of their local paper. Nothing will help your writing confidence more than to see your letter to the editor published. Cut them out and keep copies. Send them to clients, especially if your client lives out of town and does not see your newspaper. Your neighbors and local businesspeople will mention to you that they read your letter to the editor. Thank them for their kind words. You might also get letters from readers agreeing with you, or offering thanks, or disagreeing with your letter.

You might consider writing a regular letter at the same time each year, and your readers will look forward to it. For example, I have written a letter to high school and college graduates each year for the last 9 to 10 years. My first few letters were awkward, but over the years, they got better by sheer practice. This past year, a reader of my graduation letter wrote to the editor about how much she enjoyed it. She cut it out and gave it to her daughter who graduated as a single mother from a nursing school. I followed the letter up with a thank-you letter which was public in a special way.

Write a short letter on a subject such as your specialty or a local or regional problem and then offer your solution. Keep writing and try to make the letters as brief as possible. These are the ones that are read and acted upon. Your regular letters to the editor gain you a reputation locally.

The professional article published in your trade magazine will give you excellent exposure and let people all over the country and the world know about you and your specialty. This article is not only prestigious, but once your articles appear on a regular basis, your reputation will increase as well. Choose a subject that relates to your specialty area. Write a letter to the editor describing the topic and why readers will be interested in reading it. Include your resume and a brochure, with your business card. Give the editor at least 6 to 8 weeks to answer you. Do not include a copy of your article; you will wait until the editor requests it. Once you get a letter from the editor requesting it, you then send the full article. Keep a copy of the article just in case it is lost in the mail. Enclose a self-addressed, stamped envelope large enough to make it easy for the editor to send the article back to you. This is an acceptable writing policy. You can send your articles to various magazines as long as they are not in competition with one another. You can get a listing of all trade magazines at your public library or on the Internet.

Once you receive a favorable review from the editor, you will be informed of the date the article will be published and whether the magazine will pay you for it. Some professional magazines have a policy to pay in copies of the magazine; others simply publish the article but do not pay any fee. In the beginning of your practice, just getting an article in the field published is sufficient pay. You received an opportunity to tell others about your specialized field. Make copies of your article and hand them out to your clients and future clients. Ask the editor if you can tell more about yourself than just your name at the end of the article. For example, at the end of the article, it could say: Amber Wellfort is a business consultant from Medford, Oregon. She can be reached at 609 445-5692. Ask the editor to give the reader as much information about you as possible.

After the article is published, send a thank-you note and tell the editor you look forward to appearing in a future issue of the magazine.

WRITE A PUBLIC RELATIONS NEWSLETTER

To keep in touch with their clients and inform them of the changes in their field, many consultants publish a public relations newsletter. This newsletter might come out two or three times a year, and it might discuss some new clients, some new services offered by the practice, or even announce new seminars being presented by your consulting firm. This newsletter is usually given out free, and it should not be confused with the newsletter for profit, which is published by some consultants to increase their sales and profit within the firm. This newsletter for profit is discussed in Chapter 16. Some consultants are publishing public relations newsletters and to save postage costs are faxing them directly to their clients and potential clients. The newsletter business is a specialized one, and I am the author of the book, *Home-Based Newsletter Publishing: A Success Guide for the Entrepreneur,* published by McGraw-Hill, which can be ordered by calling 800 262-4729. The average public relations newsletter is $8\frac{1}{2} \times 11$ inches and two to four pages in length, on white paper, and printed in black ink. Each issue should have a theme, and each article should relate to the theme. All newsletter issues should include your full address and telephone number so people can get in touch with you for your consulting services.

START YOUR OWN CABLE SHOW

Cable television is fast becoming one of the most successful and easiest methods to communicate to people all over the world. Learn more about your local cable station and investigate what is required to obtain your own cable show to educate local and regional cable viewers about your specialty. You can do an important service to yourself as well as others. This is another low cost method to spread the word about what you offer. Call your local cable station and ask about the requirements for having your own show or even for becoming a guest on one of the various shows at the station.

DONATE YOUR SERVICES

Some professionals donate their products and services to worthwhile causes, and they receive excellent exposure for it. For example, a public broadcasting station in Boston auctions off various products and services to the highest bidder, and the money raised is given to the station to defray their costs for running the television station. They announce and show on the screen the people offering their services. For example, they will say, "Sandra

McVernon, of the McVernon Consulting Services, is offering a free seminar on Internet computer training." This is excellent publicity for any consultant for the price of a one-time service provided by you. Donate a copy of your book or a new book you recently purchased to your local public library. Once you make the donation, send a news release to the local newspaper and inform them of your donation; they will run an article on this donation for you.

PUT YOUR PLAN TOGETHER

Now that we have discussed various public relations techniques and methods, it is time to determine which ones will fit into your plans. Once you choose the best ones, use the following month-by-month listing to fill in your public relations program for the year. To get the waves of publicity, all free of charge, you must develop a year-long program and keep working the plan from January to December, year after year.

PUBLIC RELATIONS YEARLY PLAN

	THEME OR BENEFITS	TECHNIQUES
January	New researching techniques for schools	News release on new expanded consulting services
February		
March		
April		
May		
June		
July		
August		

September   _____   _____

October   _____   _____

November   _____   _____

December   _____   _____

SUMMARY

Your public relations is free; advertising costs money. Consistency is essential to your public relations success. You are the manager of your public relations program and you become the most important person in it. Ask others to give you publicity for your business. Use the news release; it really works. Get your message on the radio. Television can make you a star. Use the press kit. Sponsor a speaker; promote your own speaking engagements. Run your own public relations seminars for publicity. Teach your specialty in a class or course. Write a letter to the editor or an article on your specialty. Do a plan, and work your plan.

In the next chapter, I discuss management of your business.

MANAGING YOUR CONSULTING BUSINESS

Businesses that succeed in the 21st century are aware of the opportunities and work hard to keep their existing clients. The successful consulting businesses know that clients hire them for their particular skills to fulfill a need. As a consultant, you must deliver your services or you will be fired for not possessing knowledge and skill. The client will expect you to be an authority in your field. Your job will be not only to display this authority image, but to prove it in the real work, the assignment. Just as you must be the marketing manager in your business, you must be the operating manager as well. You have the responsibility to utilize all the resources within your command. Your consulting business will require your business skills, research skills, client relations skills, marketing skills, respect-for-clients skills, cash management skills, client selection skills, marketing-of-products skills, cash flow skills, and many other skills. Your success will be your ability to manage your skills effectively.

MANAGE YOUR CLIENT RELATIONS

Building a good, workable relationship with your clients is one of your most important responsibilities to succeed. You need your client more than your client needs you. Good client relations means putting into place proper communication techniques and treating each client courteously and with enthusiasm. Your actions are speaking louder than your voice. You are saying, "Thanks for being my client. I will work hard each day to make you my lifetime client." Your client or potential client has rights and expects certain things from you in order to continue to pay you each week or month. Figure 14-1 presents "Your Client's Bill of Rights." Review it regularly and show it to any others working with and for you.

The right to quality work from you
The right to a fair price for your services
The right to the full truth from you
The right to courteous service
The right to participate in the work assignment
The right to disagree with you and your findings
The right to object to your price
The right to demand their money back for poor services
The right to extend or suspend your services
The right to your confidentiality on their work
The right to expect you to know your specialty field
The right to expect integrity and ethical dealing with you
The right to receive the work on time
The right to make a complaint and expect a response to it
The right to expect you to fulfill your promises
The right to demand that you keep up with the changes in your specialty
The right to be treated as the *most* important part of your business
The right to prompt communication if you need an extension of time

Figure 14-1 *Your Client's Bill of Rights.*

Client relations is everything from the way you talk on the phone to the formal presentation to the client.

Successful consultants care about their clients' rights and take action when their rights are being violated. Strive to develop a client's consciousness, which means you keep looking out for your client's rights and then deliver the full benefits from your services. Client's consciousness starts before you get the work assignment and continues long after you deliver the final work. You continually ask and answer questions such as, Did I focus fully on the client's work? Was I accessible so the client could be open with me? Did I operate in a manner that helped my client get the results needed? Did I put the client's interest above everything else? Did I evaluate my full observance of my client's rights and the efforts I made daily to meet them? I like the comment from Ashley, a consultant from

Nevada, who stated, "I learned it was not what I did yesterday for my client; it was what I did today." Client relations means helping your clients daily and developing a feeling within your clients that you really care about them. Your clients become your number 1 priority and mean more than financial or business success. Once your clients are happy with your work, the rewards will become more work assignments. They will tell their friends, associates, and neighbors about you, and you will get more business for it. Good client relations cannot happen magically; it requires a 24-hour-a-day commitment and your persistence to get the results you need to succeed in your business.

KEEP TESTING TO FIND OUT WHAT WORKS

In the beginning of your business, you must try new techniques to get new clients and new strategies to retain clients, and keep improving in the delivery of your services. At a recent seminar, an engineer made a statement which many consultants or future consultants may agree with fully. He said, "I am an excellent mechanical engineer. I should be successful in my consulting business." The self-confidence you show is very important, but you must be an entrepreneur to succeed, which means you must be able to sell your services, deliver them on time, and keep your clients satisfied with you. Many skills, talents, and abilities are required to become accomplished in the field of consulting. Keep working on the various skills necessary to run your business successfully.

EDUCATE YOURSELF TO MEET YOUR CLIENTS' NEEDS

Your clients change and need new services to keep them competitive in their field. Keep a special fund, which can be called your educational development fund, and this can be used to take seminars, courses, workshops, or an educational program which can help you serve your clients better. This educational fund can help you keep up with changes in your specialty field as well. Your clients will hire you because they feel you know the current state of your field. They won't hire you because you're the field's best historian. You are expected to be on top of your field at all times, and the only way you can do this is to keep up with your lifetime continual education. You will be a student for life in the consulting business.

TEST EACH CLIENT TO DETERMINE WHETHER OR NOT IT WAS PROFITABLE FOR YOU

Nothing hurts a business more than carrying clients on the books when week after week, month after month, and year after year they are unprofitable. Profits are the lifeblood which helps run your business; losses are damaging because you spend more costs on these clients than you receive for revenue. As the owner and the manager of your business, you must regularly determine how much time was involved with each client and then determine the profit or loss. Your time is comprised of two types: one is billable, which means you can send an invoice out for it; the other is unbillable, which means that it needed to be done but could not be billed. An example might be the research you needed to do before you could start a work assignment. When you accept a new client, expect that there will be unbillable time with the first few jobs until you know the work assignments and the client better. Give yourself time to learn about your client. Try to keep all the unbillable time to a minimum. The following chart presents a monthly analysis on profits or losses for your clients. Your time is precious, and whether you bill it or not is an important cost to you because you only have 24 hours each day, and you must use your time wisely with clients who can be billed and with clients who pay their bills promptly.

The chart shows that Client A had sales of $5000 but your billable time was a total of $4000 plus the unbillable time, which might be new software you needed, or hiring extra people, or extra expenses ran up to $2000. Now your costs totaled $6000, which resulted in a loss for this client for the month. With new clients expect that there will be extra unbillable costs in the beginning, but manage them in the future to make it profitable to the client.

Monthly Profit/Loss by Client

	A Sales	B Billable Hours	C Rate Per	D Total Billable Hour Amt. (B × C)	E Total Unbillable	F Total Costs Amt.	Profit/Loss (A − F) (F + D + E)
Client A	$ 5,000.00	80 ×	50 =	$ 4,000.00	$ 2,000.00	$ 6,000.00	<$1,000.00> Loss
Client B	12,000.00	160 ×	50 =	8,000.00	1,000.00	9,000.00	3,000.00 Profit
Client C	20,000.00	300 ×	50 =	15,000.00	2,500.00	17,500.00	2,500.00 Profit
Totals	**$37,000.00**	540 ×	**$50.00**	**$27,000.00**	**$5,500.00**	**$32,500.00**	**$4,500.00**

Client B, on the other hand, had sales of $12,000 and kept the total costs in line at $9000 to gain a profit of $3000 for the month. You must continually examine not only your sales but the costs to support these sales, and try to expand your sales for the profitable clients. The more you know about each client's profitability, the better the services you can offer your clients. Watch costs but balance them with the best services possible to keep your client happy with your work. Avoid cutting back so much on your costs that your finished product is not your best work. As the manager of your business, you become the consultant's consultant, and you choose the best clients and work assignments for you.

ASK YOUR CLIENTS HOW YOU ARE DOING

No one knows how you are doing more than your present clients. Informally call your clients and ask them how you are doing. You might say, "Eddie, this is Emerson. How are things going? I know we just finished the Operation 101 a few weeks ago. Are you happy with the results and our work? I need your input." Make sure you listen carefully to the answer; your client is giving you valuable information which can help you serve your clients even better. Continue to ask clients how you are doing because it will show that you care about them and your business enough to keep wanting to improve. Keep the door of communication open with your client.

MANAGE THE WAY YOU HANDLE YOUR INQUIRIES

How do you obtain clients for your business? Did you receive the client from word-of-mouth advertising? By your direct telephone call? By a referral from another client? By delivering a speech at your local Lions meeting or professional women's club last month? By a referral from a public accountant you met at a seminar recently? Know how you attract the business into your consulting practice; you might find a thread which is affecting your business. Learn what the thread is and then use it in the future. Figure 14-2

Client's Inquiry Record

Name: _____

Address: _____

City: _____ State: _____ ZIP: _____

Telephone #: _____ FAX #: _____

Date of Inquiry? _____

What is requested? _____

Information Sent: _____

Date of follow-up: _____

How was inquiry developed   Word of   Adv   Public
                             Mouth   (News)   Relations
                             _____   Consultant   Referral (How?)

Services of interest: _____

Date put on your mailing list: _____

Comments: _____

_____

Second follow-up: _____

Figure 14-2 *Client's Inquiry Record.*

presents a client inquiry record, and you can use it to find out what marketing or public relations techniques are working to build your business. Once you find out that direct telephone calls or speaking engagements are working for you, you can do additional work in this area to increase your sales. Keep a record for every inquiry you receive whether or not you were hired by the client. Make each inquiry a part of your house list. You can send additional information in the future about new services, your newsletter, new activities in your business, or other pertinent information. Show clients how your services can benefit them.

Your inquiry might be as simple as a telephone call requesting information or a message telling you that Larry Smith, one of your clients, wants you to call. You must manage your inquiries by taking timely action to give your clients all the information they need to make a decision to hire you or at least give you an opportunity to pitch for their business. Continue to review your inquiry records regularly to determine whether you are following up promptly on inquiries and turning the inquiries into new clients. Your business will succeed when you learn to turn the inquiries into paying clients. Doing this requires you to manage your inquiry methods so you take advantage of each inquiry you receive.

The decision to hire a consultant is not an easy one for your client; it will take time and much thought, so expect some time before the decision is completed. Mary Ann, a consultant in the elderly health care field, found that many clients did not respond after her first mailing of her cover letter and brochure, but responded after sending them a newsletter on her field. Many consultants find that it takes 6 months to 1 year to get the business once the first call or mailing is made to the client. Keep in touch with your client until you get the business.

MANAGE YOUR RESEARCH ACTIVITIES

Your stock in trade in the consulting business is information; you really sell information to your client for a fee. To get the quality information required to succeed, you need contacts and people who can help you gather the best possible information to deliver to your client. Sources might be the businesspeople in your community, the professors at the local college or university, or the editor of your local or regional newspaper. Your congressman or congresswoman, the senator representing you in the Senate of the United States, and your local or state representatives are all important sources of information, as are people who direct you to the information you need. The federal government has many free publications and services for you; the only requirement in most cases will be to make your request to the right person. The important benefit of keeping close to your research contacts is that these individuals can be a source of referrals for new business. Ask to be put on the mailing lists of organizations such as governmental agencies, trade associations, business and professional organizations, libraries, think tanks, research and development agencies, and educational organizations to keep up with their latest activities and the availability of new information which can help you and your clients. Once you make a request for specific information, follow up with your contact to be certain that it is sent to you.

Figure 14-3 shows a research request log to record the research contact's name, address, phone number, fax number, date you requested information, when you received it, and date of the thank-you letter. Many consultants find that time and work can be cut when you fax the information to the contact so the work can be sent and received right away. Try to call the contact before you send the fax so he or she can watch for it and then work on it immediately. Always send a thank-you letter or, if time does not permit, drop a postcard with a quick note of your appreciation for the information. Remind your contacts regularly how much you appreciate and need their help. Send out your public relations newsletter to your contacts to inform them of your activities. The

Research Request Log				
Name of Organization and Contact	Address and Phone/Fax	Date Initial Contact Made	Date Information Received	Date of Thank You Letter

Figure 14-3   *Research Request Log.*

more they know about you and your specialty, the better job they can do for you.

MANAGE YOUR REPUTATION AND IMAGE

Once your client asks you to send a proposal for the work assignment, the decision factor may not be the quality of your proposal, your price, your experience in the field, or your presentation at the client's office. The light will shine strongly on your reputation and image in your community. Your potential client wants to be reassured that you will handle the work assignment in the most professional manner, including handling all the information you learn about the client and keeping it with complete confidentiality. All the information should be kept confidential. You must be careful about informal conversations with other business associates when you discuss your current work assignments because you cannot be certain what companies or organizations they might be working for right now. Avoid taking on new clients that are in direct competition with a present client. There may be a conflict of interest. When you are asked for information about one of your clients by a business associate or someone calling anonymously on the phone, never give out this information; it may hurt your client. Instead, tell the individual to request the information from the client directly. This way, the client can decide whether this information should be disclosed. When you know trade information about a client or a company which employed you in the past, you have an obligation to keep this confidential, much like an attorney-client relationship. Good ethical conduct means you carry yourself well, and when something doesn't sound and feel right, you do something about it. You look out for the rights of your client, and when the client can get hurt, you take appropriate action. Here are some guidelines to help determine the best action to take in keeping the best interest of your client in mind.

Treating Your Client Fairly

- Never knock your competition.
- Either say positive things about former clients or remain silent.

- Never accept a client in direct competition with a present client. If in doubt, discuss it with your attorney and your present client.

- Don't make promises to clients or potential clients you know you cannot keep in the future.

- Tell the client the truth. Lies are hard to remember.

- Treat your client the way you would like to be treated.

COLLECTION OF YOUR INVOICES IS ESSENTIAL

You need money to run your business. Many clients will hire your services and will pay you on time. Others will hire your services but will keep you waiting for payment or try to get out of paying at all. The best way to avoid this problem is to check the potential client's credit and payment history before accepting the assignment. There may be a very good reason the client was looking for a new consultant; he or she couldn't pay the first consultant.

Client XYZ was billed for $1000 for a survey you completed a month ago, and your terms are N/30, or net 30 days. You billed it out promptly on February 1, and now it's March 3 and you have received no payment. Make a copy of the invoice and prepare to call and ask for the individual you dealt with in your work assignment. Quickly review the file for the client to help you remember the assignment. Now dial the number and ask for Flora, your contact at the company.

ALICIA: Flora, this is Alicia. How are you today? I have an invoice on my desk for the survey of customers on the new software products. I noticed it was not paid. Is there any problem on it?

FLORA: There should be no problem with it, Alicia. I approved it a few weeks ago. I will check with my accounts payable department right now. Please hold the line.

ALICIA: Fine, I'll wait.

FLORA: Thanks for waiting. Yes, we have it, and the check will go out on Friday. There was a little confusion on the purchase order number, but it's alright now. Sorry about that.

ALICIA: No problem. Thanks for your help. I'll talk to you later.

By making the call yourself, you can answer any specific questions about the work that was done, the price, and any special terms on the agreement. When you have someone else call and a question comes up, you will need to call back personally to answer the question and pave the way to having your invoice paid.

Sometimes a prompt call will get the invoice paid. In other cases, it will require stronger action to receive payment. Let's say you waited a week and the check never arrived. You call again and receive another promise, but yet the check never arrives. Give Flora another call to find out what is wrong and tell her you must be paid immediately or you will be forced to take stronger action. A week later, you have not received the payment. Write a letter demanding the money, such as the letter shown in Figure 14-4.

If you fail to receive your payment by March 20, follow through on your letter to turn it over to your lawyer for collection. Never take any additional work assignments from a client who is seriously behind in payments for older work. Some consultants use the small claims court to sue clients for overdue invoices which they refuse to pay. Expect a delay to get it heard in small claims court, be prepared to defend your work, and then show that the invoice is still unpaid. My experience has shown that a lawyer who specializes in collection of nonpaying clients can collect monies faster than going through the small claims court. Call the small claims court to get copies of the summons. These are usually one page and can be filled out quickly; just make certain that the official name of the company and their address are correct before you send it.

Avoid getting negative about your clients when you have a client or two who refuse to pay you. All businesses can expect some bad debts; they are part of the territory. Fortunately, most clients pay their bills as long as they are satisfied with the work, and they pay the price which they agreed to in the beginning. When you find that more and more clients are paying very slowly, or refusing to pay their bills at all, go back and review the clients to determine if these are just new clients and this is their first opportunity to pay you. Or are the nonpayments from clients across the board—new, fairly new, and older clients—who have been with you since you started your business. Perhaps the quality of the work is not high enough, or the final proposal didn't answer their main problem, or you are taking on too much work and the quality is not there any longer. It will be easy to blame the clients, but as a consultant, you must be willing to examine all aspects of your work and try to determine what needs to be fixed to get the business and cash flow back on track.

March 15, 2005

Ms. Flora Diamendo
Marketing Dept.
GHR Company
Florida Groves, FL 11134

Dear Ms. Diamendo:

After repeated attempts to collect invoice #404 for $1000.00, we have not received your check.
This letter will serve as my demand for the $1000.00 due to me, and it must be paid by 5 p.m. on Friday the 20th of March 2005. Unless I receive payment by then, I will be forced to start legal action.

Sincerely,

Alicia Stampherst
Marketing Consulting

Figure 14-4.

TIME IS MONEY, AND MONEY IS TIME

Many of the consultants who have worked in the field for a number of years contend the most important part of their business that needs to be managed is their time. No one can manage your time but you. You must become a time manager, or you will find it very difficult to reach success in the consulting business. You have only

24 hours each day, and only 7 days each week, and you must take advantage of this time to turn out the quality work your clients deserve. Another important principle which must be addressed to achieve success is your energy. Unless you have plenty of energy, it will be a job to keep up with the demands of the business. You need energy to get the work and sell the client on your abilities to get it done, and you need energy to finish the work assignment and manage your business as well.

Each day is a new opportunity for you. It puts itself into your hands, hoping that you have learned something from yesterday, and something new about yourself, so you can set top priorities to help the most important person on this planet to you: your client.

Let's say you accepted a work assignment from the Ace Company to write a personnel manual on safety, and it will be due later this week. They agreed to pay you $2000 for it and will pay you on delivery of the work. Your number 1 priority is this work assignment, and you start it just as soon as you turn the light on in your office. There will be some interruptions, such as the phone ringing, a new fax coming in, and other normal office interruptions, but you keep coming back to your number 1 priority: the writing assignment for the safety manual. Just keep working on this project even if you are still working at 8 P.M. You are working on your most important assignment, and this has a high payoff when it's completed. Figure 14-5 is a to-do list that you can use to schedule the things you want to accomplish tomorrow. Remember to keep the important client work assignments on the top of your list. To your clients, all their jobs from the smallest to the largest ones are important.

Let other family members know that you have priorities and that your clients are counting on you. Let friends, neighbors, and former work associates know that just because you work at home does not mean you have sufficient personal time to talk with them for extended periods of time. Get into the habit of saying, "Thanks, Robert, for your call. I have a deadline on a project right now. I can talk with you later tonight or this weekend." You must protect your most important resource: your time. Keep reminding others of your priority; they will get the point. If they keep calling, screen the calls on your answering machine and phone back at your convenience. Down deep, your associates, friends, and family can understand your demand for time to deal directly with your number 1 priority.

Ranking of Items on Your To-Do List	
Rank	Item
————	————————————
————	————————————
————	————————————
————	————————————
————	————————————
————	————————————
————	————————————
————	————————————
————	————————————
————	————————————

Figure 14-5 *To-Do List.*

I have a quote taped in front of my desk at work: "Life is like wrestling a gorilla; you don't quit when you're tired; you quit when he's tired." The gorilla in the consulting business is the important work assignment which you are dealing with right now. Don't quit on it until you finish it, and this will become an important work style and important principle to help you become the best consultant in your field. Once you learn to wrestle successfully with daily number 1 priorities, you will be in training to reach your lifetime priority: to be the world's best consultant in your field. I challenge all my seminar attendees and all my students to strive to be the best and to do this by spending their time in the most important activities.

Everyone falls into small time-waster traps, which means you start on a top priority, but turn to a smaller, less important job, and the top priority gets delayed or is never finished at all. You need a time log, such as the one in Figure 14-6, and you can record your activities in 15-minute segments for the day. You will find out how you are spending your time and whether or not you are spending it for the maximum good of your clients. You might even use this as a method to bill your hours to a client.

Date ———	Name ———————		
Time	Task	Comments on Priority Number	Effective Use of Time
9:00 – 9:15	———	———	———————
9:15 – 9:30	———	———	———————
9:30 – 9:45	———	———	———————
9:45 – 10:00	———	———	———————
10:00 – 10:15	———	———	———————
10:15 – 10:30	———	———	———————
10:30 – 10:45	———	———	———————
10:45 – 11:00	———	———	———————
11:00 – 11:15	———	———	———————
11:15 – 11:30	———	———	———————
11:30 – 11:45	———	———	———————
11:45 – 12:00	———	———	———————
12:00 – 12:15	———	———	———————
12:15 – 12:30	———	———	———————
12:30 – 12:45	———	———	———————

Figure 14-6   *Time Log.*

1:00 – 1:15	_____	_____	_____
1:15 – 1:30	_____	_____	_____
1:30 – 1:45	_____	_____	_____
1:45 – 2:00	_____	_____	_____
2:00 – 2:15	_____	_____	_____
2:15 – 2:30	_____	_____	_____
2:30 – 2:45	_____	_____	_____
2:45 – 3:00	_____	_____	_____
3:00 – 3:15	_____	_____	_____
3:15 – 3:30	_____	_____	_____
3:30 – 3:45	_____	_____	_____
3:45 – 4:00	_____	_____	_____
4:00 – 4:15	_____	_____	_____
4:15 – 4:30	_____	_____	_____
4:30 – 4:45	_____	_____	_____
54:45 – 5:00	_____	_____	_____

General Review and Comments _____

_____

Grade _____

Figure 14-6   *Time Log (Continued).*

FAILURE MANAGEMENT IS YOUR JOB

A key to your consulting business will be your ability to deal with setbacks and minifailures, which will hit you in the beginning of your business and during your first few years. It will be dealing with the defeats of losing a client or of doing a dynamic presentation and finding out you were not selected for the work assignment. No one, including you, will get everything you want, and you'll have to deal with those setbacks and realize that you need them to keep building that special success, which will set you apart from others in the future. You may not realize it, but the lesson learned from a failure can make you stronger in the future when you're willing to permit yourself to keep growing.

It doesn't matter if you have lost your former job in the restructuring of the business, or you were fired, or your last business failed. Failure is a thing, not a person. In every failure, there will be some lessons to learn. Learn these lessons and move on. Debbie failed in her first business. She is just 1 of the 72,000 business owners who failed in 1994, and many will try new businesses. Debbie started her own entertainment consulting company, and when asked why the new attempt at a business, she replied, "I believe in myself, I have a lot to offer, and want to keep trying a business until it makes it." The stigma attached to a business failure or any other failure is overstated. People are much too busy and preoccupied with their own lives than with evaluating your success. I love the quote of the comic who stated, "I couldn't wait for success, so I went on without it." Go on without it, and you will eventually find it.

MANAGE YOUR CLIENT'S CONCERNS

Keep trying new methods, techniques, and ideas to get along better with your client. Remember that your client needs you, but also must approve your invoice before you get paid. Your client has a boss to whom he or she must rationalize the use of your services. For example, Jim from New York is a consultant specializing in information processing, and when he finds one of his clients upset about the services, he reacts immediately. Jim either talks to the client on the phone or sets up a meeting to discuss the problem. Jim enjoys clients, and having his own business, he also understands why the client wants to watch his costs. Jim likes to be very frank and honest with the client and expects the client to treat him in the same manner. Let's listen in on the meeting between Jim, the consultant, and Sheila, the client, in a meeting to manage the client's concerns.

> JIM: Thanks for setting up the meeting, Sheila. I wanted to talk about your concerns.
>
> SHEILA: Fine. You're welcome. Jim, I want you to know I'm happy with the new imaging system you helped us with last month.
>
> JIM: I'm glad to hear that, Sheila. Thanks.
>
> SHEILA: But Jim, I think the project took too long. Too many meetings, too many presentations, and I think we could have given you more help to speed things up. I don't think we needed all that traveling to our main office either, Jim. (Note: Jim is taking notes).
>
> JIM: Let's take one at a time, Sheila.
>
> Number 1. Time—We expected it to be done on May 30th, and we finished it June 12th because we needed to train some of your people.
>
> Number 2.—As for the number of meetings, I'll check my notes, but we agreed on the need for each meeting. I'll keep that in mind on the next assignment.
>
> Number 3. Presentations—Yes, I agree. I enjoy giving presentations. Perhaps some were not needed. I will keep this in mind.
>
> Number 4.—Travel expenses were high, I agree, but you told me yourself in our original meeting that you wanted your boss in the main office to be informed fully on the project. Would you like me to break down all the travel expenses? I would be happy to do so.
>
> SHEILA: Okay. The time is really not a big factor; we just expected it to be wrapped up earlier. Jim, we simply had too many meetings, and I couldn't get other things done during the project period. Yes, please give me a full breakdown on the traveling expenses.
>
> JIM: Thanks, I'll get the travel breakdown to you by next week. Does that time frame fit into your schedule?
>
> SHEILA: Yes. That's fine.
>
> JIM: I'm glad we talked about this, and on our next project, we can make it better for you.
>
> SHEILA: Thanks.

Communication with the client is crucial, especially at the end of an assignment if you feel the client wants to review and discuss your work. In many cases, it will include some positive contributions you made along with other things that the client wants you to handle better in the future. Be willing to accept criticism. Even seasoned consultants learn that each assignment is unique and that different solutions are needed to achieve success.

Another important time-to-manage-client concern occurs at the beginning of the job. Make certain that you know what the problem is so you can execute a good start and finish the assignment successfully. The next best time will be right after you send the invoice for your services. Your client will read the invoice and mentally ask, "Did I get my full value from this consultant? Is it really worth the price on this bill?" Your client might have to justify the cost to his or her boss. The client must believe that the value is there before justifying it to others in the office.

WALK IN YOUR CLIENT'S SHOES

You can become a better consultant when you understand the difficulty of being the client. For example, the former superintendent of schools in Boston made it a yearly practice to become a student for a day. He would schedule himself to attend six classes like all the other students at the high school. The classes included history, algebra, English, music, geography, and science. He got an excellent opportunity to observe first hand all the teachers, their lessons, and homework assignments. He even attended gym class and ate lunch with the students. This experience gave the superintendent an excellent idea of what a student could expect in a Boston high school.

Your consulting business will succeed when your clients feel comfortable with you and your work is of the highest quality. To make your clients feel comfortable, you must understand how difficult it is to be a client today. The client must define the problem, hire the consultant, and work closely with the consultant until the assignment is finished. Respect and understand the plight of the client.

MANAGE YOUR NETWORKING ACTIVITIES

The skill of putting together a system to keep the names of people who can help you in your business is priceless. Your current clients, potential clients, other consultants, other business owners, friends, family members, schoolmates from high school and college, sales representatives, associates from your various jobs, club members, teammates on sports teams, church members, former supervisors, teachers, college professors, and even neighbors should all become part of your network.

Networking is personal and nonpersonal communications with others to let them know what you do in your consulting business. It means you listen carefully to others to determine whether or not your consulting services can benefit them. Networking is essential to marketing your services because you are directly reaching out to others. Networking is built on the firm foundation of loyalty, love, and respect for others. When you receive help from someone in your network—it might be a new contact or a potential work assignment—you send a thank-you note and make an effort to give some help in return. Show your loyalty. By listening and expecting the best from others, you are showing others that you respect them. Nothing will show others you care about them more than by giving them your full respect. Expect the best from your network members. When you combine your love of your specialty field and the love you feel for your contacts and clients with the love you feel for yourself, you will succeed in your networking activities.

Tell your networking members how their work benefited you. Charlie gave you Patty's name for a potential work assignment with a plumbing contractor. You called Patty and found out the work assignment has been put on hold until next year. Call Charlie and let him know you followed it up and what results you obtained. In this way, Charlie can keep working for you. Perhaps the next time it will be more successful for you. Keep trying to help Charlie in any way you can. Show others you care.

Networking means using data bases of organizations and names, including the Dun & Bradstreet publication showing names and addresses of businesses in your area, state, and region. *The Hoover's Handbook* includes profiles of 500 major United States companies, including their products and services offered, officers' names, ages, and pay, their sales and profits for the last 10 years, their revenues by market, and their key competitors. There is a secondary *Hoover Handbook* with the same information covering major European, Asian, Latin American, and Canadian companies. These publications are available at your local or regional library. Simply ask for your reference librarian. He or she will be happy to help you network in your business. The global Internet will be one of the best networks for you into and beyond the 21st century.

Use your networking leads quickly. When you wait too long, they will be used by your competitors. Figure 14-7 shows a referral contact card. Fill it out immediately and call your new contact the same day. With the advent of laptop computers and cellular phones, you can make the communication instantly. Beat your competition to the punch by making contact as soon as possible. Once you make use of the referral contact card, add this information to your house list. Keep your communication going with this new contact before and after you're hired for the work assignment.

Manage your commitment to your target market. Once you start your business and develop an understanding of your target market, you must take the full responsibility to stay in touch, become involved, and stay involved with the needs of your target market. Never feel that marketing is not required in your business. You must strive to communicate to your target market and tell them what you offer in all your activities from marketing to public relations. You must continue to ask yourself what your target market is requesting from you. How can you make yourself shine in this market? Find ways in which you can establish yourself as the expert and important resource in your specialty field.

Contact Name _____

Address _____ State _____ Zip _____

Phone _____ Fax _____

Comments _____

Name of Network Member _____

Phone # _____

	Yes	No	Date
Sent Thank You	___	___	___
	___	___	___

Figure 14-7 *Referral Contact Card.*

A consultant has a huge ego and enjoys the challenge of tackling a difficult problem or opportunity to help the client. The client expects results, not excuses. The client wants it done today, not tomorrow. The client wants part of the credit for any successful results. When the consultant solves a problem, it's expected. When the consultant makes a mistake, everyone knows it. The consultant may wake up at night thinking about a client's problem. The consultant is a student forever and spends time with newspapers, magazines, newsletters, special reports, and the Internet to keep up with his or her chosen specialty. The consultant works in an office with four walls and tomorrow inside it. God bless the consultant.

Figure 14-8   *The Consultant.*

You establish yourself as the expert in your specialty field by being involved with your clients, by taking on difficult assignments, and by helping your clients through difficult times. Your reputation is developed by taking on the work for your target market. Each satisfied client builds your reputation for you. Please read the description of a consultant in Figure 14-8. Attending trade association meetings in your specialty, working on a panel, or speaking to your trade members adds to your following. Getting involved in any state or federal legislation that will have an impact on your specialty field will also give you added exposure.

Your target market needs to hear from you regularly in your public relations and marketing activities. Each time you run an advertisement or send your brochure and business card to a potential client, you are educating and informing new people about you. Never take these activities for granted. I recommend to all attendees in my seminar to promise themselves that they will send out 10 letters each day with their brochure and business card to potential clients or to former clients who have not requested their services recently. You must make the first move. You cannot simply wait for the telephone to ring. You must be active in your marketing activities.

MEASURE YOUR MARKETING AND PUBLIC RELATIONS REGULARLY

Never get so involved in your work that you neglect to keep those important marketing and public relations activities going. Many consultants say that 80 percent of their business will be from referrals, and your job will be to find out how these referrals were generated. Did the referrals come about from the advertisement in the trade magazine? This is the result of your marketing because you were required to pay for the advertisement. Did the referral come about when you spoke to the local chamber of commerce breakfast meeting last week? This would be the result of public relations because you were not required to pay any money for this opportunity. Once you find a positive trend that indicates which activity is generating the most referrals, you can continue this activity until it begins to slow down. Figure 14-9 presents a referral analysis. Use it regularly to keep your business growing successfully. Now let's sum up.

SUMMARY

You manage your business. Client relations is the link to your success. Know and respect the rights of your clients. Test to find out what works for you. Review your client's progress regularly. Strive

Name	Sale Yes	No	Source of Referral	Comments
Cormer Co.				
Gilda Enterprises				
Deevey Co.				

Figure 14-9   *Referral Analysis.*

to make each client profitable. Involve the clients in your evaluation of your work. Develop a system to handle all inquiries. Thank your sources for their help in your research. Put your collection method to work to keep cash flowing. Your reputation is your stock in trade; protect it fully. Time is your most important resource; you must manage it. Face up to occasional setbacks and failures. Your client's concerns come first. Keep communications open no matter what happens with your client. Find out what it feels like to be a client. Networking means getting the word out to others and letting them help you contact others. Keep working and learning more about your target market. Manage your health.

Now let's talk about your writing and the full communication skills that are essential to succeed.

COMMUNICATION TECHNIQUES FOR SUCCESS

You are an important person. Your client needs your help, but before the client will hire you, there must be a strong feeling you can do the work. One of the most important considerations for a client is the impression you make in your verbal and written messages. Successful consultants know the value of quality communication techniques to sell their services to a client successfully. Those letters, the telephone conversations, the informal discussions, and the formal presentations are important to help you make the proper impression.

Incoming communication includes the letters, faxes, e-mail, and telephone calls received by you. You cannot afford to miss any one message from your clients or potential clients. Take the example of Herbert, a California consultant. He has a home-based office and, to avoid missing calls, he installed an answering machine. The answering machine worked, but Herbert found many people didn't leave messages. He decided to hire a professional answering service so that every call would be answered by a real person and callers would feel they had talked with his assistant. Herbert personally interviewed four answering services before he decided on the one that best suited his business needs. He treats the people at the answering service very well, including gifts during the holiday season and a thank-you note when it's deserved. He keeps the answering service informed when he adds additional services or when there are any changes they need to know. Herbert feels that hiring the answering service has been very important to the growth of his business and has given him some time to work on client issues.

Watch the outgoing message on your answering machine. Once you decide on a message, check it regularly to see if it fits your business. Is it easy to understand? Does it permit people to leave their message quickly and easily? Is it a professional message? When you find that the message is no longer contributing to the image you want to project, you must make it better. Call your office occasionally while on the road and practice being a client or a potential client. Do the same with your letters and brochures; send one to yourself and open it just like another potential client. Your answering machine and your letters are gatekeepers which can open the gate to new clients or close the gates with the wrong impression.

Your outgoing communications are selling agents. Any communications you send out—from your letters to discussions on the telephone, faxes, speeches, and presentations—are very important to you. Plan your letter before you write it. What do you want to say to your client? The letter should be long enough to get your point across. It should include a beginning, which informs your reader of what you want to say, a middle, which delivers the important information, and the end, which summarizes the scope of the letter. Write about what you know. If you are unsure of something, research it fully to insure you're right before you include it in your letter. You develop your reputation by what you say, and when you develop a reputation of always checking your facts before you send correspondence out, you will save both time and money.

Speak about subjects familiar to you, and if you don't know the answer, rather than guess simply say this is outside your subject area, and when you find the answer you'll get back to them. For example, you are an investment consultant specializing in mutual funds. When you addressed a business management group, there was a question-and-answer session at the end of your program and you were asked political questions and other questions that had nothing to do with your talk or your consulting specialty. Rather than try to answer these questions, simply say, "Sorry, I would like to answer your question on foreign affairs, but this is not my specialty. I would be happy to answer any questions about investing in mutual funds." By using this technique, you are communicating the fact that you have a specialty that you want to inform them about. You are a consultant in a specialized area, and you cannot be a specialist in everything.

Good writing takes practice. Many attendees of my consulting seminars want to know how to develop writing skills to help them in their consultant practice. Practice your writing daily by writing letters to friends, letters to the editor, and letters to potential clients, clients, former clients, business associates, or new businesses. Your writing skills will increase by reading trade, business, and professional magazines. You will come across various writing styles from authors in the magazines and you will also keep up with new information in your business or specialty. The more knowledge you have in a specific area, the easier it will be to write about it. Keep looking at the information you have and develop new ways to apply and share it with others.

When you read a good article in a magazine, newspaper, or newsletter, cut it out and put it into your "good ideas for writing" file. Why did the article appeal to you? Did the writer discuss something in a unique way which brought the subject to life? Did the writer leave you thinking about the subject after you finished reading? Review those articles regularly and learn the techniques of writing which establish a credible writing style. Practicing and learning other writing styles will give you confidence in your writing. Getting an article published in a magazine or newspaper can be the confidence builder you need to improve the quality of your writing.

Use writing resources. Many consultants find that in the beginning of their practice they used standard letters to help them save time and money. There are many books at your local library or bookstore that offer standard letters for your business writing. For the small price of a book, you will have access to a wide variety of letters from a sales letter to a letter that helps you collect an overdue balance from a customer. One consultant said that by purchasing a book with standard business letters, he saved time, so he could devote more time to client's work.

LEARN THE WRITING PROCESS

Once you write a letter to your client, put it aside and reread it an hour later. Pick it up fresh. Is it clear? Does it follow through with the point you wanted to make before you wrote the letter? Does the letter have the client's interest in mind? Cut out any unnecessary words and add only words or phrases that make the letter clearer and more powerful. Print up the revised letter and review it once more for the final spelling and grammar check before you send it.

Technical words and jargon can be dangerous. Try not to use too many technical terms known by you but perhaps not known by your clients or potential clients. Some clients know the meaning of those technical words, but others are not specialists in your field. That's the reason they hired you or are considering hiring you. This does not mean that you have to remove all technical words, but try to use them sparingly until you determine that your client needs them to help you do a better job.

Good communication means responding on time. Your letter, proposal, final report, or e-mail will get more attention if it arrives at your client's place of business on time. When the letter arrives 2 weeks after you received the original letter, your client will have forgotten about it or put it at a lower priority by this time. Check your e-mail each day and respond to messages as soon as possible. If you cannot respond in detail right away, at least respond to let the client know you received the e-mail and will respond to it soon. Sometimes you can save time by making a telephone call to give the client the information requested, rather than writing a full two- or three-page letter. Some clients would rather receive the information quickly and informally than wait a long time for the formal letter to arrive. Try to avoid the reputation for falling behind in your letters or for never sending them at all. Your clients will be upset because they need information from you, and if you don't respond, they will hire someone else to get it.

DON'T GIVE AWAY FREE ADVICE

When you communicate with potential clients, avoid the temptation to give away your stock in trade: your advice. You must be paid for it in order to run your business profitably. When you first meet the potential client, it might look like you know the answer to the problem, and by offering it, you could turn the client into a client of record. But what happens when you offer the solution on the spot for free? The client takes it and never hires you. You lose. Stan, a Maryland consultant in the government selling field, avoids giving away free advice by taking notes of the first meeting so he has all the information. If the client requests an answer to the problem or some free advice, Stan will say, "I'm not sure just yet. After I review our notes, I'll be in a better position to give you the answer." Now Stan has time to review his notes and determine the answer or the advice, but he does not offer it to the potential client until he is officially hired. Stan's technique is an important one, especially for beginning consultants who are more apt to fall into the trap of giving away free advice.

Take the opportunity to close your sales. The real value of prompt, crisp, relevant communication techniques is that you develop a rapport with your clients or potential clients to sell them on you. For example, a consultant who does seminars on quality control followed up a letter from an interested potential client by saying, "Mary, our seminar in the Baltimore area is May 13th. Did you want Fred Caston and Arlene Fitzgerald to attend on that date? I can send them personalized invitations, and they can set up travel reservations." The potential client said yes, this was fine. Notice that when you show that you are helping out and giving information on time, the buyer will accept the sale. Other questions you can ask to help the client choose what is needed include: Do you want me to get started on the personnel manual for the Dallas branch? Do you want me to begin the 30-question survey or the 90-question survey for the main office in Kansas City? Notice when you show you have worked on the assignment, all you need is the approval to continue it to final completion. Ask and you shall receive the order. Good communication works in concert with your selling and marketing program.

CREATE YOUR OWN COMMUNICATION VISION

Visualize your consulting business climbing to the top of your field because of your awareness and dedication to prompt, relevant, and informative communication techniques. If you lack the time or the ability to keep up with the demands of good communication, get help from a family member if possible or hire someone who can assume this very valuable position. Once you hire someone to handle your communication needs, supervise this individual to assure that the job is being done correctly.

SUMMARY

Good communication helps you bring your services to the best possible clients. Good communication techniques help you sell better. Monitor your incoming and outgoing communication methods. Your answering machine or your telephone answering service are important selling agents. Watch your verbal communication techniques. Good writing takes practice. Get to know the writing process and use it to your advantage. Time management is essential to proper communication techniques. Watch for technical words or excessive jargon. Don't give away free advice. Create a communication vision for your practice.

Now let's talk about profitable spin-offs from your consulting practice.

PROFITABLE SPIN-OFFS IN YOUR BUSINESS

Now that you have established your specialty consulting business, there is a need to expand and include other services and products beyond the consulting services. You may ask: Why? Good question. Because with other products like articles, books, special reports, manuals, and other publishing-related products, you can be of more service to your clients. Your knowledge of your specialized field has given you a unique opportunity to share this information with others. Some will purchase your services such as advice and information; others will buy your published reports and books. Your reputation will increase in your specialized field, and you will be asked to speak to groups and organizations. Putting together various published reports, articles, and videos in your own catalog will give you the opportunity to increase your sales and your profits. These spin-offs become an extra profit center for you. The more exposure you get in various situations, such as meeting new people in your field, speaking on a panel, or sharing your expertise with others, the more your status increases. This status is worth money to you, and by offering other products like special reports and tapes, you can educate others in your specialized consulting field. Your spin-offs can help you service your field of interest.

WRITE A SPECIAL REPORT

Find an area of your specialized field in which there is some confusion or you feel people can benefit by reading a special report. For example, a consultant in the health care field just published a special report, "Strategies for Cutting Costs in Hospital Care," presented in a bright green vinyl cover. It is 24 pages long, but your special report might be only 16 to 20 pages and still do the job for you. The most important element in your successful report will be its catchy title, which tells the reader about the benefits of purchasing the report. Each report should include your name, address, and phone number so readers can contact you for other consulting services and advice. The price can be as low as $5 to $20 depending on the size and quality of the report. Some consultants will include the special report free of charge to a potential client who is interested in hiring the consultant for a major work assignment. The special report will serve to raise your reputation as an expert in your field. Here are some titles for special reports:

10 Ways to Increase Sales in Your Business

New Ways to Purchase Your Insurance

How to Motivate Your Employees with Incentive Pay

How to Train Your Employees on the Internet

How to Find a Job in the 21st Century

What Retailers Will Survive in the Next 25 Years

Before writing a report, check your magazines and newspapers to be certain that there is nothing else like it available. Your client will expect a report that is fresh and profitable to read and use. Once you have done one report, you can write others that relate to your specialized consulting field. You can sell it for $5 to $10 each, or include it in a proposal to a potential client. Revise them regularly.

SELL YOUR TAPES AND VIDEOS

The next time you speak to a management, civic, or service club in your area, be sure you take your tape recorder with you to get a tape of your talk so you can reproduce it and sell it in the future. In this way, you win in two ways: you get exposure for your talk to the club or organization and you get a chance to record your tape as well. Some people learn by listening and will purchase a tape to listen to while they drive their car or while they are working. At the end of your tapes, make certain you tell your listeners how to get in touch with you for more information on your consulting and advice services.

Sell your video on your specialized field. Today is the time for the video. People would rather see and hear about you directly in the comfort of their homes or offices. You get the chance to show your experience, your knowledge, and your enthusiasm in the field. Your video can be a public relations video in which you introduce yourself, tell the viewers about your specialized field, and give general information on some of the success stories of your practice, showing how you have helped others succeed. Tell them why you are the consultant to hire for their next consultant assignment or problem. At the end of the video, which can be 30 minutes to 1 hour, tell your viewers how to contact you. The other video to consider is a profit-oriented video designed to solve a problem for the viewer. You charge a price for the video, unlike the public relations video which would be offered for free or priced just to cover the cost of producing it. The video should have a catchy title which shows viewers how they will benefit by purchasing and viewing it. A consultant in the time management field did a video called "Winning in the Battle for Your Time." The consultant found that many people bought it because of the catchy title and the need to save time in the difficult 21st century. The price of your video can be between $15 to $20. Some consultants donate their videos to their local library or high school to get added exposure and public relations.

WRITE YOUR OWN NEWSLETTER FOR PROFIT

As you grow in the knowledge of your field and learn many new concepts from working with various clients, you can expand your client list by writing your own newsletter. Make certain that your newsletter, like all other spin-offs, restricts itself to your specialized field. Changing the newsletter to another subject will only confuse your following and hurt your marketing and public relations. Stay on track with your specialty and continue to focus on it directly. The newsletter for profit must be carefully planned and sharply focused to serve a specific target market. Your target market must have the need for your newsletter and the income to purchase it. Check the competition by reading the *Directory of Newsletters*, which can be obtained at your local public library. Purchase a sample copy of each newsletter in your specialized field. Determine how your newsletter will be different and how its content will help your readers. Make certain that you have the time to devote to your newsletter before you decide to start it. Your clients come first in your business. Give yourself sufficient time in your practice to learn your business and understand your clients well before you take the responsibility for starting a newsletter.

People will purchase your newsletter when they feel that the information it contains is worth the price of a yearly subscription. You can succeed in your newsletter when you include only hard-to-get information not available in the newspapers or magazines that people in your specialized field regularly read. Make certain that you monitor each issue of your newsletter to make certain that only new and relevant information is offered.

You can publish the newsletter on a monthly, bimonthly, or quarterly basis. The price you charge can be from $18 to $100 each year, depending on the quality of its contents, and the income of your target market. Your current client list might be an excellent starting point for potential subscribers. Attracting a subscriber is difficult, and sometimes it can be even more difficult to have the subscriber renew the subscription annually.

A common question I receive from seminar attendees is whether or not they can hire a writer for their newsletter. The answer is yes, as long as you are certain that the writer knows enough about your specialized field. You must supervise the newsletter completely and review all material before it gets printed and sent out to your subscribers. Once you decide on publishing your newsletter, take the full responsibility to make it work for you. You are the manager of all your consulting spin-offs.

BECOME A PAID SPEAKER

This can be one of your most important spin-offs, which can increase your reputation and earn you extra money. Write to various clubs, associations, and organizations that hire and pay for speakers and inform them of your availability. Follow up with a phone call a week later and then send a tape, a video, and a photograph to show that you want to be their speaker. As a beginning speaker, you could expect $300 to $400 per speech. As you develop experience, you can expect $500 to $1000 per speech. Ask to have your travel costs paid. Consider hiring an agent who can get you additional speaking engagements but will charge you a commission of at least 15 percent. To become a top speaker, you need as much experience as possible to make each speech better than the one before it.

Choose a subject for your speech that will offer a rapid solution to a problem, show others how to succeed, or how to make more money. Everyone is interested in making more money at work, getting a better position, and getting along better with other people. Here are some potential speech topics to offer your favorite group:

How to Manage Your Career

How to Start Your Own Business

How to Motivate Your Sales Force

How to Increase Profits in Your Business

How to Write a Marketing Plan

Using Your Most Important Resource: Your People

Saving and Investing for Your Retirement

How to Switch Your Career and Succeed

To make extra money as a speaker, you need to keep promoting yourself, your qualifications, and your ability to entertain the audience. There is an excellent book, *Secrets of Successful Speakers*, published by McGraw-Hill, to help you learn all the steps to become a topnotch speaker.

RUN YOUR OWN PROFITABLE SEMINARS

As you learn how to speak successfully to groups, you are preparing your skills for running your own seminars. A seminar usually runs from a half day to 2 full days and includes handout material for attendees to take home. You use a teaching style to present a seminar successfully. They are excellent tools to show others your expertise in your field, and some of your attendees will become clients.

Choose a catchy, relevant topic from your consulting specialty. Next write out a brochure describing the seminar and the benefits attendees will receive from it. You can charge $99 for a half day, $150 for a full day, and $199 for 2 full days. Choose a hotel or convention center near your home to hold your first seminar. Make sure you schedule the seminar before you list the date and starting and ending times in your brochure. Mail the finished brochure to your house list, some of your clients, former clients, and potential clients that will be interested in attending. Don't make the mistake of setting up seminars in six major cities before you get the experience and knowledge from the first and second seminars. Seminars are very tiring both physically and mentally. Try to keep your seminar schedule limited so you can focus on your clients' needs. Some potential seminar titles are:

Time Management for You

Stress Management in the 21st Century

Research Techniques Using the Internet

How to Purchase a Country Business

Project Management in Today's Business

Marketing Your Services Today

Public Relations Campaign Techniques

Human Resources Management

The Internet in the 21st Century

Expanding Your Small Business

Businesses for Misplaced Employees

Keep testing your seminar titles, prices, mailing lists, locations, format, and length until you get the combination that works for you. Once your seminar program has grown extensively, you can hire a seminar company to run it for you.

PUBLISH YOUR OWN BOOK

Many consultants are establishing themselves by writing a book to showcase their expertise and experience in their specialized field.

In Boston, a consultant in the area of change in the workplace wrote a book that sold thousands of copies and reached the best-seller list. Many consultants mail out review copies to business publications, which have subscribers who are in a position to hire the services of the author-consultant. Choose a subject that will reinforce your specialty field and at the same time show meaningful benefits to the reader. Some consultants write books to show that their specialty is a global subject and is not restricted to the United States or Canada. For example, Chuck is a consultant specializing in exercise and fitness, and his book shows how other countries view exercise and fitness and how this information can help everyone. Susan is a consultant in the domestic violence field, and her book shows how various cities, states, and institutions such as schools, churches, and local governmental agencies deal with this growing problem in today's world. Your book will be an important learning tool for everyone in your target market, and this is a way to reach people who might never meet you.

RESEARCH WHICH BOOKS ARE SELLING STRONG RIGHT NOW

Before you write your book, take some time and visit your favorite bookstore to see what books have already been published in your specialized field. For example, a consultant in the area of business wanted to write a book on motivation, but when he went to the bookstore, he found volume after volume on this subject. After talking with the bookstore manager, he decided to write a book on how to reward employees successfully, and this book turned out to be a bestseller. Many businesses want to know how to reward their employees in ways other than putting more money in their paychecks. Take a new look at your specialty and determine meaningful subjects for books which will fill a special need. Some excellent topics for nonfiction books include health care, inspiration, multicultural relations, aging, resume and career, and business and fitness. Your success with your book will require both good content and marketing. You must believe in it to make it sell. You must also believe in it right from the start in order to sell it to your publisher. Write some potential titles on a sheet of paper. Narrow them down to two or three of the best. Now choose the title that offers the most benefits to your readers. Here are some potential titles for a book on helping others get a job in the difficult working world:

The 10 Best Strategies to Get Hired

How Winners Get Jobs Today

Finding a Temporary Job Today

Superselling Your Skills

How to Interview Like a Pro

Finding the Hidden Job Market

Once you choose the best possible title which will utilize your interests, skills, talents, and abilities, you are ready to do your first selling job. Sell your idea to a publisher to get it published. This is called a query letter, and it includes three basic parts: an introduction of the title and concept of the book, the full description of the target market you want to purchase it, and why you should be the author of the book. Discuss why you and you alone are the best person to write the book. This includes your background, your previous jobs, your consulting experience, and how you have helped clients in your specialized field. If you have other publishing credits, such as magazine articles, manuals, or newspaper articles, mention them in the query letter. Include your most recent resume. Send this letter and resume to a publisher that specializes in this field. You can find publishers' names in your local library, bookstore, or in the *Writer's Market* book (Writers Digest Books), which is updated yearly and offers a list of hundreds of publishers of various books from business to education, medical care, sports, hobbies, and women's subjects. If you don't hear from the publisher in 6 to 8 weeks, drop them a note. If you don't hear for another 3 weeks, send your query letter to another publisher. Never call on the phone because publishers receive thousands of query letters. Never feel discouraged. Winners never quit; quitters never win. Believe in yourself and your potential book idea.

Once the publisher writes you a letter expressing interest in your idea, you will be asked to submit a proposal that gives the publisher more information to make a decision. The proposal includes a summary of your work, an outline of each chapter, and descriptions of your target market and other people who would buy your book. You may also include a copy of your resume and any other articles you have published in magazines or newspapers. Let the publisher know that as an expert in your field you will be at an advantage in writing the book. Discuss fully why you should be the person who will write this exciting book. Give the publisher at least 8 weeks to review your book proposal before you call or write. The publisher will then hand your proposal to the editor in charge of your subject area, and if the editor likes it enough, it will be brought up at an editorial meeting. At the editorial meeting, the publisher, editors, and marketing staff discuss your proposal for the book. This meeting is similar to a group of people within a company deciding whether to hire you as their consultant.

Within 3 months after you send your proposal, you should hear from them. They will either send you a letter telling you that the proposal is excellent, and a contract will be sent to you shortly. Or you will receive a letter expressing thanks, but informing you that they cannot accept your proposal at this time. If you are turned down, remain positive. Writing is a difficult world, and you must keep trying. With the contract in your hand, you need to be a good time manager to write the book and still keep all of your clients happy with your quality services. Once the book is published, you will be a celebrity, you will attend book signings, your clients will want an autographed copy, and your reputation will soar at the same time.

How much money can you expect to make from your book? Since this is your first book, you will have to develop a reputation as a selling author before you start to earn substantial income. You will receive a modest advance between $2000 and $10,000 for your first book, and it will increase with your success. You will pay back the advance with royalties, which are usually 7 to 10 percent on books sold. The real value of being a book author will be the publicity you gain as an author in your specialty field.

There are alternatives to using a commercial publisher. Publishing is a very difficult field, and many consultants cannot find a publisher for their manuscripts or book ideas. Another option is to become your own publisher, whereby you write the book, let your hired editor do the editing, proofread it, and then have it printed by your own chosen printer. This is called a self-published book. In this case, you keep all of the profits, and when you sell a book for $15 and your cost is $8, you earn a profit of $7. It will be up to you to do your own marketing and distribution of your book. Some consultants hire a small publishing firm to help them market and distribute their self-published books.

MERCHANDISE YOUR CONSULTING AND SPIN-OFFS INTO YOUR OWN CATALOG

I wrote a book on mail order, and one of the most important concepts I tried to impart to my readers is the importance of developing a line of products or services. Since you have started your specialty consulting business, you need a technique to keep getting new clients to replace the ones that leave, die, move away, or simply switch to another consultant. A catalog is a small book, leaflet, or file containing names, articles, and listings. It can be four to eight pages long or as large as necessary to show your client what you do and what you have to offer them in your specialized field. Your catalog should be planned and include only the services and products that will educate, entertain, and motivate the readers to act and then buy from you. With your own catalog, you are not restricted to the Cleveland area, the Portland area, or the Dallas area, but now you can communicate to the whole country and the world on what you have to offer.

What should you offer in your catalog? Present yourself and your excitement for your specialty field. It doesn't mean just listing your consulting services. You could give valuable information about developments in your field and letters from readers discussing your specialized field. You can tailor your catalog to reflect your personality, passion, and enthusiasm for your specialty. The role of your catalog is to show your readers that you're fully absorbed in your field by helping your clients, writing about it, and conducting seminars and research in your field on a permanent basis. By putting together a catalog and distributing it to others, you give your readers an opportunity to read it and purchase one of your articles, books, or videos and then consider becoming one of your clients. The catalog becomes the stage to showcase your business. It becomes a consulting store that you can send to the businesses and homes of your clients or potential clients. It will be the marketing tool to keep telling new people about you. Never grow tired of telling others about yourself. You are the number 1 product, and you must keep selling yourself and your services to succeed. Here is a list of possible contents of your consulting catalog.

CONTENTS OF YOUR CATALOG

1. Letters from readers
2. Letters of recommendation from clients (get their approval first)
3. Worksheets or charts
4. Copy of your resume
5. List of government agencies involved in your specialty
6. List of your special reports, books, articles, videos, directories
7. Upcoming seminars schedule
8. Newsletter description and information on how to order it from you
9. Price list and order blank to order other material from you

I enjoy including a small inspirational article in my catalog. I have a consultant friend in the investment field who includes a retirement worksheet to help her readers determine how much savings are needed to reach their retirement goal. Other consultants include letters from their clients discussing the difficulty of being a client and how to get the most for their fees. Be willing to give your catalog reader important information to help discover more about the field, including resources such as the names of federal, state, and local governmental agencies. Susan, a desktop publishing consultant in Pennsylvania, asked a consultant in another specialty to share her house list so she could mail her catalog and reach new people to share her specialty field. Another consultant in Massachusetts shows photographs of attendees of his recent seminar. A picture is worth a thousand words. Some consultants include information in their catalog about their newsletter and offer a discount if the readers subscribe within 10 days. Include the products that you feel will benefit your readers and make the catalog-reading experience a beneficial one for your readers. Consider putting your catalog on the Internet.

FIND A WAY TO TRACK THE CLIENTS YOU DISCOVER AND SELL WITH YOUR CATALOG

For example, let's say you do a mailing of your catalogs, and Sam Smith, who is a potential client, writes to you and orders a special report. Six months later, you make another mailing, and this time Sam buys one of your books. Keep a list of how you obtained the client so you can use this same technique to get other clients. You might find a successful thread. Your success in this business will be to develop ways to reach, sell, and sign up quality clients. Many of your future clients will read your catalog and then think about buying one of your products. Once satisfied with your knowledge of the field, they will then hire you as the consultant of record.

PRODUCE AND SELL YOUR OWN DIRECTORIES

Some consultants learn their specialty field so well that they become familiar with all the key players in the field all over the country and the world. Knowledge of the field can help you make money putting names, addresses, and resources into a directory. People will pay $25 to $150 for a unique, difficult-to-find directory of your specialty field. Some fields are so new that the demand is strong for directories. Keep the size of your directory to a minimum so you make a reasonable profit while still offering a service to the readers in your specialty field. Keep the directory updated so you can continue to sell new editions.

SUMMARY

Writing articles and reports can be an excellent way to show your knowledge to potential clients. Produce your own video while speaking to a local service or business group. Paid speaking engagements help you pay your bills but force you to improve your speaking skills. Seminars for profit help you meet and share your passion for your consulting specialty. Put out your own specialty newsletter and charge a subscription price which reflects your experience. Publish your own book. Choose a catchy title and be willing to promote the book widely to make it a success. Clients enjoy bragging about their consultant who just wrote an exciting book. Put out your own catalog including information on your advice and consulting services and the various spin-offs such as articles, special reports, tapes, videos, and books. Your catalog can be the marketing tool you need to succeed. Some consultants include information in their catalog or their newsletter and offer a discount if readers subscribe within 10 days. Include in your catalog the services and products you feel will benefit your potential clients. Compile and sell a directory of resources in your specialty field.

SUMMING UP

Congratulations to you for reading this book. At this time, I would like to offer you the important points that can help you establish a successful consulting business. The key to success is your willingness to put in the time and effort and to deliver the best possible results for the most important person: your client.

WHAT YOU NEED TO SUCCEED IN THIS BUSINESS

1. You will be able to use your skills, talents, and abilities in an exciting way.
2. You will be helping your client solve problems.
3. You must put your client first.
4. You need to learn to run your own business.
5. Your success will result by being a partner to your client.
6. Your success will depend on selecting the best possible specialty field.
7. You will be successful when you match your skills to your chosen field.
8. The most successful consultants focus on their specialty; you can do the same.
9. Spend your time learning your field better than anyone else.
10. Learn the consulting process and keep using it for each client, whether big or small.
11. Your success is in one word: *competence*.
12. Save your excuses; your quality work will be the building blocks for your success.
13. Take the time to get to know your clients.
14. A consultant offers advice and information for a fee.
15. You need to earn fees to stay in business.
16. You need to earn a profit to stay in business.

17. Never give away your advice or information for free.

18. Take assignments and projects you want and feel you can do well.

19. In this business, you sell your time; you must learn to be a time manager.

20. You must manage your resources to succeed.

WHY SHOULD YOUR CLIENT HIRE YOU?

21. Your client will hire you only when he or she feels you can make an important contribution or solve a problem.

22. You will have competition in your business; show your client why you should be hired instead of your competition.

23. Make a list of what factors your client will use to evaluate you before hiring you (review Chapter 11).

24. Review the benefits you offer to your client (see Chapter 12).

25. Be willing to go the extra mile for your client.

26. A successful consultant is an educator.

27. Your clients need your skills, your experience in the field, and your ability to get things done.

28. You have the power of information to help your client.

29. Your role will be to help the client save time, effort, and money.

GETTING YOUR HOME OFFICE ORGANIZED

30. By proper office organization, you can turn out the best possible work.

31. Your clients need not know you work out of your home.

32. Make a list of the equipment and furniture essential for your office.

33. Choose a room which can hold this equipment and furniture and give you maximum privacy.

34. Consider purchasing used furniture and equipment or renting it in the beginning of your business.

35. Do an office layout.

36. Get quality stationery and business cards.

37. Purchase supplies you will need to save time.

38. Get the necessary business permits for your area.

39. Choose the best business organization.

40. Hire an attorney, accountant, and insurance agent.

41. Your accountant can tell you what needs to be done financially to succeed. Profits are essential.

42. Set up your office space so it can be used 24 hours each day.

43. Set guidelines for other family members.

44. Remember that in the home-based business, the word *home* comes first.

How to Choose Your Specialty and Reach Your Clients

45. You must know what you offer your clients and set a priority to reach your marketing niche.

46. Spend time reviewing your personal inventory (Chapter 4).

47. Your life and work experiences are important to your success.

48. Give yourself full credit for your past experiences.

49. All experiences—good and bad—help you.

50. Review all possible consulting fields. (Appendix B)

51. Choose the best field for you.

52. You must assume the responsibility for reaching your clients.

53. Develop and use your 30-second elevator speech.

54. Find your target market and direct your energies to reach it.

55. Learn the demographics and psychographics of your market.

56. Never take the competition for granted.

57. Markets change, and you must change to serve them.

58. Review the numerous target markets.

59. Match your specialty to your target market. This is what will make you successful.

60. Consider groups such as accountants, teachers, and business owners, which can give you referrals.

61. Set your marketing strategy.

62. Gather information on your potential clients to help you sell.

63. Nothing happens until a sale is made at a profit.

64. The telephone connects you to valuable potential clients.

65. Move the client from being a prospect to being a client of record.

66. Set a sales quota and work to reach it.

67. Selling is a 24-hour-a-day, 7-day-a-week process.

THE CONSULTANT PROCESS FROM BEGINNING TO END

68. Know your competition fully.

69. Call potential clients to get your appointments.

70. Write personal letters and follow up.

71. Develop rapport with your potential client.

72. Work on getting referrals.

73. Make the best possible impression on your first meeting.

74. Keep good records of all communications.

75. The contracting meeting is your selling meeting.

76. Get as much information from your client as possible.

77. Submit all bids to your potential clients.

78. Your proposal opens the door for the sale.

79. Avoid giving away advice or information for free.

80. Follow closely the statement of work.

81. Pricing must be fair for you and the client.

82. Include your resume or other information which will sell your services to the client.

83. Make sure each job is a profitable one for you.

84. Keep making presentations, even when you are turned down.

85. Accept the client's decision.

86. Take any defeats gracefully; you might be hired later.

87. When you are awarded the job, write a thank-you note.

88. Get a signed agreement before you start the job.

89. Contracts are subject to changes and adjustments.

90. Keep all contracts in a safe place.

91. Plan the work assignment carefully.

92. Develop a strategy and work the strategy.

93. Take the action to succeed on the job.

94. Expect fears and nervousness.

95. Use your information resources.

96. Bring the job to completion.

97. Make the final report as professional as possible.

98. Know your material, the audience, and your findings.

99. Present your findings with clarity and confidence.

100. Each presentation makes you a better speaker.

MARKETING AND PUBLIC RELATIONS TECHNIQUES

101. You are selling a service to a target market.

102. Learn your marketing mix fully.

103. Know your product mix, pricing mix, promotion mix, and distribution mix.

104. Marketing and public relations work together.

105. Marketing is a 12-month-a-year process.

106. Advertise regularly in print publications.

107. You are the marketing manager, and you position your services.

108. Public relations is publicity for free.

109. Your news release is your most important publicity tool.

110. Challenge yourself to get more public relations.

111. Appear on radio and television to gain exposure.

112. Speak at every chance you get.

113. Run a public relations seminar.
114. Teach and write about your specialty.
115. Start your own cable show.
116. Write out a marketing and public relations plan.

MANAGE YOUR CONSULTING BUSINESS

117. Pay attention to your client relations.
118. Keep testing your results.
119. Handle each inquiry completely.
120. Manage your research activities.
121. Your reputation and image are essential to your success.
122. Monitor your cash flow; keep collections steady.
123. Manage your time use.
124. Expect your share of failures and setbacks.
125. Keep communication open with all clients.
126. Manage your networking activities.
127. Watch all incoming and outgoing communications.
128. Create your own communication network.

PROFITABLE SPIN-OFFS FOR YOU

129. Sell publications in your specialized field.
130. Offer tapes and videos.
131. Become a paid speaker.
132. Offer profitable seminars.
133. Publish your own book and promote it.
134. Develop your own spin-off catalog.
135. Happy selling. Work hard to keep your clients and make your business a success.
136. *Good Luck!*

32 IDEAS TO INCREASE SALES IN YOUR CONSULTING BUSINESS

1. Pass out business cards regularly.
2. Write letters to the editor.
3. Run your own seminars on your specialty.
4. Give away a half hour of consultation free.
5. Become a guest on a local cable show.
6. Speak at your local Women's Professional Club.
7. Print your own brochure and hand copies of it out.
8. Inform other professionals in your field about your services.
9. Review your sales and client assignments.
10. Join an organization or club in your field.
11. Write a magazine article about your specialty and send it out to clients.
12. Tell others about success stories of your clients.
13. Keep telling others about what you do using your 30-second elevator speech.
14. Call or write current, past, and potential clients.
15. Start a newsletter about your specialty.
16. Speak to a class at your local high, junior high, or vocational school.
17. Start or join a network group of consultants from various fields.
18. Use e-mail and the Internet to keep your name in front of your market.
19. Keep telling others what contribution your benefits make to your target market.

20. Get listed in printed directories and bulletins.

21. Send out regular mailings to your house list.

22. Make presentations to current clients to resell them on your services.

23. Enter or start your own trade show of consultants.

24. Set a quota of sales leads each week. Make appointments. Sell, sell, sell.

25. Review your customer service program to maintain and resell current clients.

26. Use news releases to get free publicity.

27. Talk regularly with former employers, associates, friends, and classmates in your field.

28. Review other services, such as selling reports, books, and paid speaking assignments, to increase your sales.

29. Never permit sales leads to go stale. Send them a brochure and/or sales letter, and then follow up by phone for an appointment.

30. Run your promotion selling program all year long.

31. Review your progress regularly; keep using the techniques that are working for you.

32. Join a consulting association in your field.

SPECIALTY CONSULTING FIELDS

Accident investigation

Accounting and auditing

Acoustics

Acquisition and mergers

Advertising

Aeronautical engineering

Agriculture

AIDS—Health services

Air conditioning

Air pollution

Animal care

Appraisal and valuation

Aptitude testing

Arts and administration

Asbestos handling

Assertiveness training

Association management

Audiovisual services

Automation and change

Banking and finance

Behavioral sciences

Biotechnology

Budgeting and planning

Building property management

Business and financial ventures

Business brokerage

Business plans

Business services

Cable TV

Camp selection

Career development

Cartography

Catering

Change management

Chemical engineering

Child care programs

City planning

Civil engineering

Commodities trading

Communications

Community relations

Compensation planning

Computer graphics

Computer programming

Computer security

Computer technology

Computer tech—Desktop publishing

Computer tech—Software programming

Computer tech—System analysis

Conference planning

Conservation

Construction management

Construction management—Building maintenance

Construction safety

Consulting

Consumer information

Copyright law

Corrections facilities

Crisis management

Cross-cultural relations

Curriculum development

Customer service

Demographics

Dental management

Direct marketing

Document analysis

Downsizing

Drug and substance abuse

Drug testing

Earthquake engineering

Ecology

Economic research

Editorial services and writing

Education services

Electrical engineering

Electronics

Employee benefits planning

Employee selection

Employee surveys

Energy management

Entrepreneurship

Environmental issues

Ergonomics

Estate planning

Ethics

Executive development

Executive search and recruiting

Export-import

Facilities design and management

Factory management

Family business

Family relations

Financial management

Fire investigation and protection

Fleet management

Food processing and managing

Foreign language translation

Forensics

Forestry

Foundation management

Foundry technology

Franchising

Fraud investigation

Freight management

Fund-raising development

Futures trading

Genealogy search

Geology

Geotechnical services

Golf course design

Government regulations

Graphic design

Hazardous waste material

Health services

Historic preservation and restoration

Home health care

Hospital administration

Hotel and motel management

Human resources

Humor

Image marketing

Immigration and naturalization

Industrial engineering

Industrial psychology

Industrial safety and security

Information systems and data bases

Insurance and liability

Interior design

Internet computing systems

Interpersonal skills development

Inventory control

Investment counseling

Investment fraud

Labor relations

Landscape architecture

Land use planning

Language skills training

Leasing

Legal services licensing, patent, and copyright assistance

Library management services

Literacy

Lithography

Lobbying

Logistics

Mail order

Maintenance management

Management

Manufacturing and industrial operations

Marine engineering

Marketing programs and services

Marriage and family relations

Materials handling and engineering

Materials technology

Media buying

Media presentation skills

Media relations

Mediation and arbitration

Medical equipment

Membership development

Mining engineering

Motivation training

Museum design and management

Music
National safety programs
Natural resources
Needs assessment
New product marketing
Newsletter production
Noise pollution
Nonprofit-related programs
Nuclear engineering
Nursing
Nursing home administration
Nutrition
OSHA
Office management
Oil and gas exploration
Operations research
Opinion polls
Organization analysis
Organization managerial starting
Packaging
Participative management and personnel
Pension planning
Performance appraisals
Personal image
Personality testing
Petroleum engineering
Pharmaceuticals
Philanthropy
Photography
Planning—Long-range
Planning—Short-range
Plant and office layout and design
Plant security
Plastics technology
Political processes
Pollution control
Preretirement planning
Problem solving
Procurement
Product design and evaluation
Production evaluation
Product liability
Productivity
Profit sharing
Program and policy development
Project management
Protective coatings
Psychological counseling and testing
Psychological services
Psychology
Public affairs
Public relations
Publishing
Purchasing
Quality control issues
Radio
Rail transportation
Real estate
Records management

Recreation planning

Recycling

Reliability management

Religion

Research and development

Retail distribution

Retail sales

Retirement planning

Risk management

Robotics

Roofing

Rubber technology

Safety engineering

Salary administration

Sales management and training

Salvage and reclamation

Sanitation

Sanitation—Management

Sanitation—Wastewater
  management

Security

Shipping

Site analysis

Small-business development

Social services

Soil and site analysis

Solid waste management

Space planning

Special education

Sports

Statistical process control

Strategic planning

Stress management

Structural engineering

Substance abuse programs

Supervisory development

Surveys—Internal and external

Systems analysis

Tax planning

Team building

Technical writing

Telecommunications

Telemarketing

Television, cable TV, and radio

Terrorism—Protection services

Textile technology

Theater management

Time management

Total quality management
  (TQM)

Toxicology

Traffic and parking

Training and development

Transportation management

Travel and tourism

Trustee services

Turnaround management

Urban renewal

Utilities management

Valuation and appraisal

Value-added reseller

Venture capital

Video production and
audiovisual services

Vocational training and
rehabilitation

Volunteer management

Wage and salary administration

Water pollution

Water systems management and
distribution

Weather forecasting

Wellness programs

Wholesale sales

Wildlife management

Wind energy

BASIC CONTRACT FORMS

CONTRACT

This contract is made on _____ , 19____ ,
between _____ ,
residing at _____ City of _____ ,
_____ State of _____ , and _____ ,
_____ residing at _____ ,
City of _____ , State of
_____.

    For valuable consideration, the parties agree as follows:

    No modification of this Contract will be effective unless it is in writing and signed by both parties. This Contract binds and benefits both parties and any successors. Time is of the essence of this contract. This document, including any attachment, is the entire agreement between the parties. This Contract is governed by the laws of the State of _____ .

The parties have signed this Contract on the date specified at the beginning of this contract.

_____   _____
(*Signature*)   (*Signature*)

_____   _____
(*Printed name*)   (*Printed name*)

TERMINATION OF CONTRACT

This Termination of Contract is made on _____ ,
19___ , between _____ ,
residing at _____ City of _____ ,
_____ State of _____ , and _____ ,
_____ residing at _____ ,
City of _____ , State of
_____.

For valuable consideration, the parties agree as follows:

1. The parties are currently bound under the terms of the following described contract, which is attached and is part of this Termination:

2. They agree to mutually terminate and cancel this contract effective on this date. This Termination Agreement will act as a mutual release of all obligations under this contract for both parties, as if the contract has not been entered into in the first place.

3. This Termination binds and benefits both parties and any successors. This document, including the attached contract being terminated, is the entire agreement between the parties.

The parties have signed this Termination on the date specified at the beginning of this Termination.

_____   _____
(*Signature*)   (*Signature*)

_____   _____
(*Printed name*)   (*Printed name*)

MODIFICATION OF CONTRACT

This Modification of Contract is made on _____ , 19___ , between _____ , residing at _____ City of _____ , _____ State of _____ , and _____ , _____ residing at _____ , City of _____ , State of _____.

For valuable consideration, the parties agree as follows:

1. The following described contract is attached to this Modification and is made a part of this Modification:

2. The parties agree to modify this contract as follows:

3. All other terms and conditions of the original contract remain in effect without modification. This Modification binds and benefits both parties and any successors. This document, including the attached contract, is the entire agreement between the parties.

The parties have signed this modification on the date specified at the beginning of this Modification.

_____   _____
(*Signature*)   (*Signature*)

_____   _____
(*Printed name*)   (*Printed name*)

EXTENSION OF CONTRACT

This Extension of Contract is made on _____ , 19___ , between _____ , residing at _____ City of _____ , _____ State of _____ , and _____ , _____ residing at _____ , City of _____ , State of _____.

1. The following described contract will end on _____ , 19___:

This contract is attached to this Extension and is part of this Extension.

2. The parties agree to extend this contract for an additional period, which will begin immediately on the expiration of the original time period and will end on _____ , 19___.

3. The Extension of this contract will be on the same terms and conditions as the original contract. This Extension binds and benefits both parities and any successors. This document, including the attached original contract, is the entire agreement between the parties.

The parties have signed this Extension on the date specified at the beginning of this Extension.

_____   _____
(*Signature*)   (*Signature*)

_____   _____
(*Printed name*)   (*Printed name*)

19 POINTERS FOR STARTING YOUR SUCCESSFUL CONSULTING BUSINESS

1. Review your list of the benefits you can offer your clients.

2. Reread your inventory of your interests, talents, and abilities.

3. Choose the best consulting specialty for you.

4. Take smaller assignments at first, which you can handle while holding down a full-time job.

5. You are the consultant, owner, marketing manager, and a very important person for your clients.

6. Focus on quality not quantity of work.

7. Strive to turn a client into a raving client, who will give you many referrals.

8. With each success, you can add to your assignments, client list, challenges, and move your business into full time.

9. Believe in what you do, put your client first in your business, and enjoy yourself fully.

10. Each day ask "What did I do today to help my clients?" Show your clients you care with your actions.

11. Expect and deal directly with setbacks and problems.

12. Balance your life. Work hard, play hard, and carve out a personal life for yourself.

13. Manage time, stress, and yourself.

14. Stay current in your specialty field. You are the dean of your own university. Be a student forever.

15. Keep telling others about your specialty, your success stories.

16. Autograph your brochures and give them out regularly, with your business cards.

17. When the client hires you it means you owe the client your hard work to give your best.

18. You are only as good as your last assignment.

19. The world needs you. Go forward and serve your clients. *Good luck.*

INDEX

ABOUT THE AUTHOR

William J. Bond has spent the last 30 years studying, researching, and writing about successful people in home-based businesses and in the world of work. He has conducted lectures and seminars across the country. His book, 1001 Ways to Beat the Time Trap, *was chosen by* Publishers Weekly *as a major book of the year and was a selection of the Money Book Club.*

His popular Home-Based Business *series has shown thousands how to successfully operate mail order, catalog, and newsletter businesses from home. With Going Solo, he adds home-based consulting to this series.*